Beginning

One of the strange things about living in the world is that it is only now and then one is quite sure one is going to live forever and ever and ever

Frances Hodgson Burnett, The Secret Garden

R emember that time you looked around your home and, with sudden dismay, thought, 'I have too many houseplants'? Us neither. Because when it comes down to it, life with a potted plant is undeniably better. And better yet is the ability to grow and replicate new, healthy houseplants without ever having to visit a garden centre again. To share, swap and celebrate the miraculous methods of multiplying all of your favourites at almost no cost at all.

And here's the secret: it's really, really easy.

Plants are designed to multiply. They spread their roots, send off inquisitive shoots and regenerate themselves in all sorts of exciting and unexpected ways without any help. Even for the beginner indoor gardener, a single leaf can hold enough life to be successfully grown into a brand new plant.

Perhaps you've already filled your home with potted plants and are wondering, what's next? Or you've seen a favourite tropical plant burst into bloom and suddenly outgrow the space you've styled for it in your home. Rather than simply prune it back, it is possible to use existing leaf and stem material to duplicate and produce exact clones, genetically at least. This is called asexual or vegetative propagation, and it requires no pollination or germination. In fact, just about every houseplant you've ever owned (or dreamed of owning) can be multiplied in this way.

There are certain plants that will present miniature clones of themselves as if by magic, such as the seemingly immortal spider plant. There are others that need a little more planning and encouragement, but which are just as amenable to producing new, replica plants. All you need is a few straightforward techniques, the right environment for your new plant family, and just a touch of patience.

With the help of this book, you'll quickly discover how to take cuttings, cultivate runners and offshoots, divide plants at the roots and even grow brand new root systems in the air. You'll learn pruning methods that produce no waste, organic recipes, and eventually enjoy gifting and swapping newly grown greenery with friends, family and other houseplant hoarders you might meet along the way.

You will also discover DIY projects to better nurture and display your plant family, including a homemade propagation chamber and a simple self-watering planter.

Ultimately, we hope that we can help you view the plant life you come across on your everyday adventures in a new light: with the potential to become new plants and be transported to new places. Namely, your home.

Understanding Propagation

About a year ago, Rose rescued a damaged – but particularly pretty – succulent from a local gardening fair. The scrawled writing on its tag simply read: 'mother of thousands'. Huddled neatly around the fringe of every leaf were row upon row of plantlets, each a tiny replica of the parent plant, many of which, on closer inspection, had happily flung themselves onto the surrounding compost. Long story short, we now own a lot of mother of thousands (*Kalanchoe daigremontiana*) plants.

Propagation is the way in which plants reproduce, and there are two types: sexual or asexual – the latter is also sometimes called vegetative propagation.

Sexual propagation in plants involves seeds. It starts with pollination and, later, germination. It requires the meeting of two different sets of genetic information (the pollen from the 'male' plant and the reproductive organs of the 'female' plant) and results in a brand new, genetically unique offspring. It's a bit like human reproduction, but with more bees and squirrels involved.

For the casual indoor gardener, the specific conditions – and very long wait times – required can make experimenting with seeds seem a little bit daunting. What most people ideally want is to be able to propagate their plants without too great a risk of failure.

Plants are magical because they contain cells that can easily grow into other parts; for example, the stem of a plant can produce roots, while a tiny portion of leaf or root can create stems. This is what asexual propagation – and this handbook – is all about: easy, inexpensive and generally faster techniques for expanding your plant family.

Asexual methods of propagation are also wonderful for their spontaneity; there is nothing better than being able to bring a little piece of a plant home, whether taking a cutting from a foreign plant discovered while travelling (with the permission of the owner, of course), or being gifted a precious offshoot from a relative, friend or neighbour.

There are so many reasons to learn about propagation: more (free) plants; plants with a backstory, and therefore more personality; and, perhaps most importantly, a way to connect with the natural world. For many, the emotion bestowed upon these organic forms as they grow, thrive and flourish often goes much deeper than a superficial need for something beautiful in your home, however valid or appreciated that might be. Plants and flowers embody progress, optimism and even our urge to celebrate a simple love of life.

Whatever the plant you'd like to propagate, our detailed propagation table on page 97 should help you determine which method of propagation is best-suited to its needs. It lists many of the houseplants we have come to know and that we've found people love best, together with the most successful propagation methods for each plant.

Useful Terms

Aerial Root
A root that grows in the air to seek out support or nutrients

Activated Charcoal
A form of ground charcoal used to filter harmful bacteria and toxins from water

Active Growth Period
The period when a plant grows new leaves and flowers, typically between early spring and late summer

Asexual Propagation
Producing new plants using existing material from the parent plant. Also known as vegetative propagation

Coir
A fibrous, absorptive material made from the husk of coconut shells, often used as a rooting medium

Compost
Used in this book to refer to different growing mediums. These are usually composed of an organic medium (such as coir) plus sand, vermiculite or perlite, and sometimes added nutrients

Dormant Period
Between the end of summer and start of spring when plant growth is inactive

Family
A family is a group of plants which contains one or more genera

Genus / Genera
A classification of plants within a family, containing one or more different species

Hydroponics
Growing and raising plants by feeding them with a mineral nutrient solution in either water or a compost-free medium

Node
The point on a stem where new leaves or buds grow

Offset / Sucker
An offshoot growing along or below the soil line of a plant's main stem

Perlite
Lightweight expanded volcanic glass used to assist drainage in compost

Petiole
A stalk that connects a stem to a leaf

Pinching Out
A form of pruning that involves removing the growing tips or young side shoots to encourage fullness

Propagator
A transparent box, sometimes heated, in which seeds or plantlets are grown

Rhizome
Underground stem that grows laterally and can send out roots and shoots

Sexual Propagation
Reproducing plants using seeds or spores

Species
A set of plants within a single genus, with similar characteristics and the ability to interbreed

Succulent
Any plant that has adapted to store water in its leaves and stems, which are often juicy and thick

Vermiculite
A mineral used to assist drainage and retain nutrients and moisture in compost

Tips for Successful Propagation

1
Choose plants that are healthy and pest free, unless as a last resort

2
Propagate during a plant's active growing period (this is usually spring or summer), and before midday if possible

3
Fertilise the plant several months before you intend to start propagating

4
Water the plant to be propagated a day or so beforehand; this is particularly important for succulents

5
Ideally collect rainwater or use distilled water to quench your plants. Let it come to room temperature before watering

6
Take more cuttings than you need, as some (sadly) may not flourish

7
Keep cuttings at a suitable temperature – consider providing bottom heat during colder seasons by using a heated propagator or heat mat

8
Reuse old materials, such as glass jars, plastic bottles and takeaway boxes, which make brilliant drainage trays

9
Always make sure tools and equipment are clean, from your cutting knife to your container

Tools
& Materials

Knife
If you can invest in a specialist grafting knife (usually affordable), you will create cleaner cuts and reduce tissue damage. Otherwise, one that is very sharp, sterile and non-serrated will do the job

Knife Sharpening Stone
To keep your knife and secateurs in top condition all year round

Secateurs
Handy for pruning and taking cuttings from large, woody stemmed houseplants

Scissors
These are indispensable for cuttings and general pruning

Spoon
A simple, everyday tool for potting and transferring seedlings

Pots
Young roots do not require a lot of space to grow, so go small rather than big. We find 8cm (3 inch) plastic gardening pots work well for most single cuttings. Most importantly, ensure good drainage

Rooting Chamber
Find or design one that works for you. See pages 30–35 for inspiration

Seedling Trays
Go for fairly shallow trays and make sure they have drainage holes

Tray Tamper
A smart little wooden block which knocks the air pockets out of seedling trays and pots

Capillary Mat
An absorbent roll of material that provides a steady supply of water to young cuttings and seedlings. Used as a lining in a watering tray, the mat prevents damage that can occur from under- or overwatering. You can buy one from a garden centre or experiment with a towel or piece of wool felt

Sticks / Canes
Collect an assortment of bamboo canes and wooden skewers for various propping needs

Clear Plastic Bags
These act like brilliant lids to seal in humidity. Re-use wherever possible

Twine / String / Elastic bands
For all your twisting and tying needs

Watering Can
We prefer the plastic type with an adjustable nozzle for fine misting

Small Chopping Board
Essential for making leaf and stem cuttings without damaging surfaces

Spray Mister
We prefer the plastic type with adjustable nozzle

Leather Gardening Gloves
To protect your hands from sharp tools and prickly cacti

Ecothrive Charge
A fertiliser we love, made from the droppings of organically reared beetles

Best Watering Methods

Taking care of the parent plant is vital when you want healthy offspring. And it's important to treat propagated plantlets particularly gently as extreme watering, temperature or lighting can quickly kill cuttings and offsets at their delicate, early stages.

So when you first bring a plant home, start with a little research to determine its natural habitat. This will help you to replicate its light, temperature and watering preferences as best you can. Often we care for a plant a little too eagerly without being sure of its needs, and the most common killer is, tragically, overwatering.

This is unsurprising considering that many of the prettiest houseplant containers don't have drainage holes. If a plant sits in excess water then the delicate hairs on its roots will be damaged, inhibiting their ability to absorb moisture and nutrients. This is why you often see a waterlogged plant looking sad and droopy.

It is therefore essential to your plant's long-term health that there is space between its roots and the bottom of its pot – you can achieve this by choosing a pot with a drainage hole, or by adding a layer of drainage stones at the base if it is sealed. A sprinkle of activated charcoal in among the drainage stones will help to filter out any harmful bacteria.

A layer of topdressing stones is beneficial too; this will not only trap humidity, but will also reduce algae growth on cacti and other succulents and prevent flies laying eggs in the compost.

For all houseplants, rather than watering as a matter of strict routine (which ignores the changing conditions of different seasons), we recommend developing a habit of checking each plant's compost with a fingertip inserted to a depth of about 3–5cm (1½–2 inches).

We tend to do this once a week on a Saturday or Sunday, and set up a timer on our phones as a reminder.

Tropical plants (including jungle cacti) like their compost to remain moist, but never soggy. We find that watering balls (refillable glass or plastic globes that can be stuck into the compost vertically to release water gradually), help to control water intake and reduce maintenance without drowning the plant. If watering as normal, only ever water a tropical plant once the top 3cm (1½ inches) of compost feels bone dry.

Desert-dwelling cacti and succulents prefer the occasional generous watering, followed by a period of drought. So allow the soil to dry out completely and only give them a drink once the compost is dry throughout.

In either case, if you feel any dampness, hold off watering and check again the following week. And always empty a plant's drainage tray a few hours after watering.

Using rainwater is hugely beneficial, as it avoids the calcium damage that can be caused by the limescale found in tap water. You can place a bucket outside your home and decant the water into your watering can; your plants and plantlets will be so much healthier for it.

Aim to use room temperature water (you can leave it standing in the can for a couple of hours). And to avoid dislodging often rootless plant material, water either from below or with a fine misting spray attachment on your watering can.

It is also best to water in the morning when the plant is most active – this allows moisture to be effectively absorbed and ensures a well-quenched plant.

Recycling & Reducing Waste

The issues of mass production and wastefulness are more apparent than ever before – and like almost all of our friends and customers, it is something that plays a huge part in our everyday decision-making.

Multiplying and swapping homegrown plantlets is so much more rewarding than buying them. Instead of buying plants (with little knowledge of the impact their journey to you has had on the planet), you can create brand new plants with virtually no negative impact at all.

Propagation is a wonderful way of reducing waste in other ways, too: rather than disposing of healthy pruned stems, you can easily turn these cuttings into new plants to give as gifts (or, er, simply hoard). Propagation can even help save a favourite ailing plant from the bin; taking a healthy cutting or offset from a plant that has been attacked by mealy bugs, for example, is a chance to resurrect it in a fresh life form.

Plastic is a difficult material to avoid, even in the gardening industry. For us, the key is to try to be as resourceful as possible and repurpose materials in inventive ways to reduce the needless purchase of more plastic. We find the packaging that mushrooms and fruit are sold in make brilliant drainage trays; glass or plastic bottles work perfectly for rooting cuttings in water; and jam jars are just the right size to experiment with germinating tropical fruit seeds.

Make sure to give everything a thorough clean with hot, soapy water and rinse thoroughly with clean water before use. This ensures any harmful bacteria is banished and the soap is washed away.

We believe that growing your own greenery is an essential way to combat some of the limitations and stresses of city life, giving a sense of true accomplishment. If we take the time and care to minimise our impact, that sense of accomplishment becomes even greater.

Rooting

**Life begins the day you start
a garden**

Chinese proverb

The Ideal Rooting Environment

Controlling the environmental conditions (see the list opposite) of your newly propagated plant will increase the likelihood of healthy growth and significantly speed up the rooting process. It is especially helpful to any newly cut plant parts which have a limited ability to replace lost moisture, needing a bit of help until they have established new root systems. It is also essential if your home is below the ideal rooting temperature (approx 21°C / 70°F), particularly if you are propagating during colder months of the year.

A practical rooting chamber will help control all of the elements listed opposite. Many of the step-by-step techniques included throughout this book require a rooting chamber of some sort, whether that be a shop-bought propagation unit, individual pot and plastic bag, repurposed container or a homemade mini greenhouse – for inspiration, see pages 30–35. We recommend experimenting with a few to find a design that works best for your needs; as long as it is sterile, stable and provides good drainage, it should do the job.

Remember to treat propagated plantlets very gently – don't subject them to any extremes in moisture, temperature or lighting, and disturb them as little as possible during the first few months.

Moisture

We've outlined the best watering practices on pages 18–21, but one of the keys to good moisture is good compost. You want a nutrient-rich compost that is light and supports the plant properly, and which also stays moist and allows good drainage. If that sounds like a lot to manage, do not fear! You can use our simple homemade rooting compost recipes on page 40, which provide a base for retaining the right level of moisture.

Humidity

Tropical plant cuttings will benefit from a humid atmosphere which is as close to their native environment as possible. You can increase humidity by covering the cuttings with a transparent cover such as a cut-off bottle or plastic bag, but make sure you allow small holes for air circulation. Desert cacti and succulent plantlets won't require a cover, since they will successfully root with much lower levels of humidity.

Light

Most newly propagated plants require plenty of bright, indirect light. If sunlight becomes too strong (scorching leaves or drying them out), temporarily cover the plant with some sort of translucent shade, such as a sheer fabric or wax paper. If you don't have enough natural light, you can experiment with grow lights, which we have found to be really effective. These work best when used with tropical cuttings and seedlings.

Temperature

The most critical factor for rooting is the temperature of the compost. Generally speaking, a consistent room temperature of 21°C (70°F) is ideal, and no lower than 12°C (54°F) at night. If your home is cooler than 15°C (59°F), you could invest in a heated propagator to increase humidity and regulate an ideal temperature. We recommend investing in one which includes a thermostat to ensure it does not get too hot; many cheap models are prone to overheating. Watering with room temperature water will help to regulate this, too.

ROOTING CHAMBERS

I f plants make people happy, and getting your hands dirty is the key to feeling connected to the natural world, then we like to think of a homemade rooting chamber (or miniature greenhouse, as we think of ours) as the root source of green-fingered happiness. They're cheap as chips to make, too.

There is more than one way to make an effective rooting chamber, so rather than featuring step-by-step instructions and photos of one design, we have included photos throughout the book of many different homemade rooting chambers and shop-bought propagation units, which we hope will inspire you to improvise and have fun with the materials you already have in your home and garden.

The size of your new plantlet is one of the first things to consider. Basic plastic storage boxes are great for larger cuttings, while smaller plastic fruit and salad boxes make brilliant mini-propagation units for growing seedlings.

You also need to consider the cover: if you decide to keep things simple with a standard plant pot as the base, you can use a cut-off plastic bottle as the lid, or a clear plastic bag propped up with a rigid support like a short length of bamboo cane.

Bear in mind that drainage holes are necessary, allowing you to water any delicate plantlets from below without disturbing them or ending up with soggy compost. (If it is impossible to add drainage holes to your base vessel, we recommend watering little and often with a spray mister, and adding a layer of drainage stones below the compost to act as a reservoir, which should prevent rotting roots.)

To help you identify the best spot in your home to set it up your new rooting chamber, make sure to read the information on pages 28–29, which explains the ideal light and temperature conditions for optimum rooting.

Wooden or plastic container, at least 5cm (2 inches) deep – this could be a shop-bought seedling or rooting tray
Scissors
Compost (see p40)
Tray tamper (optional)
Spray mister
Large transparent plastic bag or the cut-off base of a plastic bottle
A few handfuls of small drainage stones
Thin bamboo canes, wooden sticks or other rigid supports
Grow light (optional)
Twine, string or bin bag tie

1 Prepare your materials by giving them a thorough clean and rinse to remove any bacteria. If you are using drainage stones taken from the outdoors, give these a wash too.

2 If your repurposed container doesn't have drainage holes, use some scissors or a skewer to puncture it with plenty of small holes. Then fill your base with compost, patting it down gently with your tray tamper to remove air pockets. Spray the surface of the compost with water so that it is moist to the touch, but not soggy.

3 If you're using a plastic bag as a cover, open up the bag and lay it down sideways so that the opening faces you horizontally. Scatter a layer of drainage stones at the bottom of the bag to create a reservoir for excess moisture. Carefully slide your container inside, sitting it on top of the drainage stones.

4 Trim the canes or wooden sticks to around twice the height of the cuttings you intend to take, around 20cm (8 inches) minimum in length. Insert one stick in each corner of the container so that they stand securely upright. These will support the plastic cover and stop it drooping down and disturbing the plantlets. If the sticks refuse to stay upright, try resting a large-ish stone against each one to prop the sticks into each corner.

5 Make some small cuts in the roof of the plastic bag to allow air circulation. For most propagated plant material, it is best to keep the miniature greenhouse away from direct sunlight to avoid drying the compost out. If you are using a grow light, you can now position it roughly 30cm (12 inches) above the rooting chamber. Check the particular propagation methods described later in the book to learn how best to treat different cuttings.

6 Once you come to placing new cuttings inside, you can either use the twine, string or bin bag tie to seal the open end of the plastic bag, or alternatively you can tuck the loose plastic underneath the bottom of the container. This will allow easy access when it is time to water. You will know when to water by testing the moisture level of the compost with a clean fingertip. It should feel damp but never saturated. If you think the compost is too dry, use your spray mister to squirt water into the layer of drainage stones rather than watering from above.

7 Try not to disturb the rooting chamber too often during the first few months, but ensure there is enough air circulation to prevent mould forming. If any plantlets look rotten or turn yellow during the rooting process, you can carefully remove and dispose of these areas to reduce the chance of the mould spreading.

Hardening Off & Potting On

'Hardening off' is the process of acclimatising young, recently rooted cuttings to their surrounding environment. It is carried out gradually to prevent shock from sudden changes in conditions.

A couple of months after planting cuttings or plantlets, look out for signs of new growth – you should begin to see new shoots develop on the stem or from the compost around your cuttings.

At this point, you can begin to harden off the plantlets by opening up the plastic bag which they are encased inside – do this incrementally, gradually increasing their exposure time over a period of days. If your chamber lid is rigid, you can do this by propping it up with a stone. As long as the plantlet remains looking healthy and doesn't wilt or change colour, you can be confident that it is happily acclimatising.

When you are ready to transfer each plantlet into its own pot, begin by watering the compost around it with a spray mister. Very gently scoop the plantlet and its surrounding compost out with your fingers or a spoon, and transfer it to a newly prepared pot, securing the new compost around to keep it supported.

Keep the repotted plantlets in the same position as your rooting chamber for at least a few weeks to make sure they experience no sudden changes of light or temperature. After a few more weeks, you can transport them to a new spot. If they show signs of suffering, such as wilting or changing dramatically in colour, reconsider their needs and, if necessary, give them another period inside the rooting chamber until they are more mature.

Rooting Boosts

Most parts of a plant already contain growth hormones that will spring into action when required, ready to help it develop new roots.

So while it isn't always essential, we often use natural rooting ingredients to promote faster root growth. These act as a catalyst and have antibacterial properties that encourage the process, ultimately increasing success rates. Sadly, it's inevitable that some cuttings will fail, so always take more than you need.

Certain plants – such as succulents, which are happy to root in even the most unlikely conditions – have no need for the use of a rooting hormone. Others – such as thicker, woody-stemmed species – will benefit hugely.

We tend to avoid shop-bought rooting powders. Those marketed as 'natural' are often largely talcum powder, and others contain synthetic chemicals that are unappealing, especially when treating edible cuttings such as herbs. However, they are effective and convenient, and are perfectly fine to use if you prefer.

If you do opt for a shop-bought rooting powder, avoid sticking the cut stem straight into the container – which can cause cross-contamination if any bacteria are present on the cutting – instead, remove a small amount of powder using the end of a knife or spoon. Also avoid getting the powder anywhere other than on the very tip of the cutting end – always tap off any excess. Using too much can actually inhibit root growth.

Cinnamon

Ground cinnamon has the benefit of being a mild fungicide and protects cuttings from the growth of fungi or bacteria. Directly after taking a cutting, simply dab a little cinnamon on to the tip of the cut end before transferring it to your rooting compost.

Many believe cinnamon makes a good natural pesticide spray. To try this, boil some water, transfer to a small jug and allow it to cool to a warm temperature. Then add 1 teaspoon ground cinnamon. Leave the mixture to infuse overnight. The next day, strain it into a spray bottle, then mist the stems, leaves or compost of ailing plants.

Raw Honey

Honey is another natural antibacterial ingredient that some believe also contains enzymes to promote root growth. Dip cut stems into a little raw honey before planting in your rooting compost. You can also dissolve honey in freshly boiled water and, once cooled, add the brew to cuttings rooted in water or compost to give them a little boost.

Willow Tea

The enigmatic willow tree is shrouded in mystery and folklore, and has been the source of homemade remedies since medieval times. The bark of the willow tree is known to be antifungal and contains a high level of rooting hormones.

To make a natural rooting brew, take cuttings from the youngest shoots of any tree from the willow (*Salix*) family, aiming for around six or so 10cm (4 inch) pieces. Remove any leaves and trim the stems down to 2–3cm (¾–1 inch) pieces. Add these to a jug of freshly boiled water, and leave them to soak for a couple of days. Strain the willow tea into a storage bottle and store in the fridge or in a cool, dark place. Use within 1 month.

To aid propagation, simply dip the raw tips of your stem cuttings into a little of the tea (we pour a couple of teaspoons out into a bottle cap first), or moisten a layered cutting with a few drops using a pipette.

Homemade Rooting Compost

It's important to use a specific compost when planting cuttings, since root growth requires a sterile environment, with good drainage and a bit of breathing space.

As a base, the coir in these recipes works by retaining a good level of moisture. The vermiculite or sand creates space for the roots to breathe.

Make as much as you need for the potting or planting you're doing. We like to pick a day to pot lots of plants at once, making a mix up in a large plastic box so that any spare can be kept for later – store it somewhere cool and dark. We find a cup is a handy measuring tool.

When potting up, you want the compost to be patted down so that it is fairly firm but not packed too tightly. This is to make sure the cuttings will not shift around, but still have enough air circulation. You can use a 'tamper' to knock the air pockets out, or simply tap the pot gently on a hard surface a few times.

For repotting or dividing a plant that already has an established root system, it is best to use a similar compost to the original, since plants generally don't like being moved from one compost to another, very different one. This isn't the case for cuttings or other rootless offshoots, which are more adaptable.

If you prefer, there are plenty of other propagating composts to be found online and in garden centres. Look out for organic, peat-free blends, which are more environmentally friendly.

Tropical Houseplant Cuttings & Rootless Offshoots

Rock dust and worm castings contain essential minerals, each adding long-lasting nutrients to this compost that should enrich the plant's health.

7 parts coir
1 parts worm castings
2 part vermiculite
Pinch of rock dust (optional)
Sprinkle of Ecothrive Charge (optional)

Combine all the ingredients and mix well. For repotting and dividing tropical houseplants, increase worm castings to 2 parts.

Cacti & Other Succulents

This medium is suitable for all succulent repotting and propagation purposes.

1 part coir
1 part horticultural sharp sand or perlite

Combine the ingredients and mix well. If repotting, remember the importance of drainage – make sure you have drainage holes, or add a base layer of stones and a teaspoon of activated charcoal.

Rooting in Water

Rooting a cutting in water is probably the easiest and most affordable method of propagation, and there is no better way of making use of your old jam jars and pots.

All plants need oxygen, water and nutrients to survive, along with some support in the form of a rooting medium. With traditional indoor gardening, this is normally compost, sand, coir or some combination of these. Nurturing plant growth in water, or 'hydroculture', eliminates the need for a rooting medium, with the plant drawing oxygen and supplemented nutrients from the water, and support from the vessel.

Some plants that will successfully root in water include vines such as English ivy (*Hedera helix*), golden pothos (*Epipremnum aureum*) and heartleaf philodendron (*Philodendron scandens*), wandering Jew (*Tradescantia pallida*), dumb cane (*Dieffenbachia*), begonias and species of *Rhipsalis*. Herbs such as basil, mint and rosemary grow brilliantly in water too.

When taking a stem cutting, cut just below a node – you can find out more about this in Step 2 on page 58. It is best to remove any leaves lower down the stem that will sit in water and encourage the growth of bacteria. And remember to refresh the water at least once a week to prevent algae growth. You could use a water-soluble rooting aid (see pages 36–39) to speed up rooting process, along with a teaspoon of crushed activated charcoal to cleanse the water.

When it comes to choosing your vessel, choose any that is watertight; an opaque container will reduce algae growth, meaning you need to refresh the water less frequently, but we prefer using clear glass jars so that the developing roots are visible. We find that watching this remarkable stage, which is normally hidden, makes the process feel even more magical. We also recommend choosing a vessel that is not too big, since the cutting will release vital rooting hormones and these are most effective when undiluted.

Don't miss our Root Chutes project on page 64 to help you prop your cuttings up.

You can leave your cutting to grow in water long-term and the advantages of this are worth considering: by eliminating the compost you remove the source of pest and bacteria growth, and – joy! – you never have to worry about under- or overwatering the plant again. With the occasional addition of liquid feed, the plant will simply draw as much moisture into its stems as it needs.

If you begin by rooting a plant in water, but don't intend to nurture it long-term in this way, you'll need to be a little more proactive. Cuttings rooted in water will naturally produce aquatic roots, which look and act differently to roots grown in compost, since they are specially adapted to absorb oxygen from the water. Therefore, it is essential that you transfer the cuttings into pre-moistened compost before the roots grow to more than a couple of centimetres (an inch or so) long. Don't worry if the roots outgrow this length while in the water, as you can simply trim them back and wait for them to reach the optimum length again.

To pot them, make a hole in the compost with your finger or a pencil to minimise root damage, otherwise the plant will be unable to function properly once potted up and will most likely wither and die.

Cuttings

I often painted fragments of things because it seemed to make my statement as well as or better than the whole could

Georgia O'Keefe

R ose and I are always on the lookout for unusual species to add to our expanding houseplant collections. Rather than simply buying a mature plant, it's much more satisfying to take a small cutting to nurture and grow yourself, especially if it's been gifted from a loved one.

Equally rewarding – and essential for us, to keep our jungle studio from being taken over completely – is having people visit us and take cuttings home themselves. It is always inspiring to be sent a photograph down the line of a familiar, flourishing plant that has been successfully transported from one home to another.

When people think of taking cuttings, they often imagine simply trimming off a leafy stem and sticking it in compost – which can be a really effective method – but lots of houseplants struggle to grow new roots in this way. Those with tougher, woody stems such as *Dracaena*, *Yucca* or rubber plant, root slowly and are susceptible to disease unless they are looked after in very precise conditions.

That's not a problem, though, as there are all sorts of basic cutting methods that are suited to different families of houseplants, each utilising a unique section, from root to leaf tip.

Each plant contains hormones to allow it to root and grow, and these hormones are found in differing concentrations depending on the area of the plant. Newly growing shoots contain significantly more hormones than more mature stems, so it is easier to take cuttings from these younger and therefore more active areas. Younger shoots are often a brighter and lighter, verdant green colour, and are often found lower down, or around the outside of the plant, where they branch outwards.

That said, older stems can be propagated from too; they just need a little extra preparation and might take longer to root. This is good news, since it is often thin and leggy, or old and rebellious stems that you might want to trim back to improve the shape of a plant, especially if you have chosen the plant to liven up a confined space like a shelf or work desk. Pruning and pinching older sections will also stimulate fresh growth in a mature plant, so taking stem cuttings is always beneficial. More about making the most of pruning can be found on page 170.

Each of the cutting methods in this book will describe exactly when, how and where to take your cuttings. As general advice, remember to water the plant the day or two before you plan to take cuttings if possible, and if you can give it a feed a few weeks or so before, you'll be giving the cuttings the best chance of producing a healthy new root system. The process of rooting can also be much more successful with the help of a rooting ingredient – more information about these can be found on pages 36–39.

Stem Cuttings

In terms of speed, stem or 'softwood' cuttings are the best way to multiply your plants, and they make brilliant gifts as they don't take long to establish. There are so many houseplants that can be multiplied with this technique, including most branching succulents, forest cacti, vines and larger tropical genera such as *Monstera* and *Dracaena*.

Pruning and shaping the stems in this way is mutually beneficial for you and your plant – not only do you create a new plant for your collection, but by reducing its size, the parent plant will respond by triggering new shoot growth in other areas, eventually becoming fuller and stronger. With a leggy succulent, for example, you can cut the entire main stem off to be planted as a cutting, leaving behind a comical looking stump. As if by magic, the stump will callous over, and often two strong new stems will develop from its sides, eventually leaving you with two vigorous succulents.

If you have a stem cutting, but don't have time to plant it straightaway, you can root it in a jar of water to begin with. Just bear in mind that the stem must be replanted in compost as soon as the roots begin to show. This process is explained in more detail on pages 42–45.

If you come across a plant on your travels that you are desperate to take a stem cutting from, but you can't pot it up immediately, give it the best chance of survival by keeping the cut end wet. To do this, wrap the tip of the stem in tissue soaked in water and then cover the tissue in a layer of watertight tin foil. Alternatively, you can carry the stem home in a plastic bottle filled with a few centimetres of water, remembering to give it some air, as well as the right temperature and lighting it needs, on your journey home.

Tropical Stem Cuttings

Pots and drainage stones
Tropical Houseplant compost (see p40)
Spray mister
Sharp, sterile knife, scissors or secateurs
Rooting boost (see p36–39)
Dibber or pencil
Rooting chamber (see p30–35)
   or propagation unit

To establish a fuller plant you can root more than one stem in a single pot. Or, if your cuttings are fairly large, like the *Monstera deliciosa* pictured here, use one or two individual pots. If propagating a plant cutting that includes very large leaves, you can conserve moisture by trimming the outer edges of these leaves away.

To read more about the rooting process, choosing the perfect spot to place your cuttings and information on hardening off once rooted, flick to page 35.

1 The soft stems of tropical plants will lose their moisture quickly and are susceptible to airborne bacteria, so begin by preparing your pots so that you can transfer the stems as quickly as possible once cut.

Start by lining your drainage trays with small stones and fill your pots with fresh, pre-moistened rooting compost. Use your tray tamper or just tap the pots gently on a hard surface to get rid of any large air pockets. Dampen the surface of the compost with a few sprays of water.

2 Next, choose the stems you wish to propagate. Very mature, thick stems can take much longer to root and are therefore more likely to fail. It is best to pick stems that are young and bendy, but at the same time mature enough that they would not snap if bent.

Cut more stems than you need in case some don't root. To identify where to cut, look out for the 'nodes' – these are the points along the main stem where side stems and shoots grow (see example image on page 52). Using a clean knife or scissors, make a cut just below a node, which is the spot where rooting will take place.

3 Leave some leaves at the top of your cutting, but if there are any surplus leaves or side shoots along the main stem, pinch or trim these off to allow the cut end of the stem to be easily inserted into the compost. This will also help to direct as much energy into rooting as possible.

4 Remove a little of your chosen rooting boost on the end of a clean knife or spoon. Gently coat the surface of the stem's cut. Try to avoid getting the rooting boost anywhere other than on the very tip, and, if using powder, tap off any excess before planting.

5 Make a hole in the rooting compost with a dibber, finger or pencil to a depth of about halfway inside the pot – just deep enough to hold the stem up securely. Stick the stem into the pot, and push some compost around it to secure it.

6 Place each pot on its drainage tray inside a plastic bag and loosely seal each bag with string or a bin bag tie. To finish, cut some holes for air circulation.

The cuttings will stay here while they take root, which could take anywhere up from a few weeks, depending on the conditions.

Succulent Stem Cuttings

Sharp, sterile knife, scissors or secateurs
Pots, trays and drainage stones
Cacti & Other Succulents compost (see p40)
Sticks or canes (optional)
Spray mister
Rooting chamber (see p30–35)
   or propagation unit

The structure of trailing succulents' stems, particularly those of the *Rhipsalis* genus, can vary significantly from species to species. If obvious nodes (the points along the main stem where side stems and shoots grow) are not visible, try the leaf blade cutting technique on pages 91–93. In this step-by-step, we've used *Epiphyllum phyllanthus*.

   If you have a very leggy succulent that needs reviving, first pluck off all the lower leaves and set them aside to be propagated using the Succulent Leaf Cutting technique on pages 84–87. Then sever the top portion of the plant (with some leaves still intact at the top), and plant this shorter stem in fresh compost (using the method below), where it can produce new growth as a succulent stem cutting.

1 Identify your nodes (the point that new shoots grow), then take your stem cuttings at an angle with one clean chop, cutting at least three nodes, or 10cm (4 inches), below the leaf. Just below the node is where roots will appear, so aim for the final trim to be here.

2 When taking cuttings from a cactus, succulent, or other very juicy plant, the cut end must be allowed to callous over before planting to avoid bacteria getting into the stem. Leave your cuttings indoors on a clean, dry surface away from direct sunlight for a minimum of three days to a week.

3 Once the cut ends have hardened, prepare your pots. Remember that you can root more than one succulent stem in a single pot to establish a fuller plant. Fill each pot with fresh compost and tap them on a surface to remove any air pockets. Line your drainage trays with drainage stones to allow excess moisture to escape after watering.

4 Next, plant the stems. Push the cut ends into the compost until they are deep enough to stand unsupported. You may need a stick or bamboo cane for longer cuttings, or some wire or hairgrips to anchor heavier trailing succulents like the burro's tail. If you are propagating a finer-stemmed succulent like a *Rhipsalis*, you can plant more than one stem around the inner edges of the pot, which will give them something to trail over.

5 Moisten the surface of the compost generously with your spray mister, and then it's all about aftercare.
   Water the cuttings periodically, every three weeks to a month, and only when the compost feels completely dry throughout. Avoid direct, hot sunlight while the stems are rooting. Only move the new plantlets into more sunshine once you know they have established new roots. You will know when they have taken root by pulling upwards very gently on the stem, and feeling for any resistance. If the stem shifts, replace and leave them for another month at least. If you feel resistance, you know rooting has begun.

ROOT CHUTES

S ince there aren't many products on the market to aid rooting in water, we started making these simple clay funnels to support our sprouting stem cuttings and seedlings. We were inspired by the artist Michael Anastassiades and his 'Floating Forest' series, and our friend (and talented ceramicist) Bridget McVey helped us refine the chutes to make them watertight. Since no kiln is needed, it's the perfect project to try with kids.

Although glass vases do look beautiful as a base, you don't have to use a transparent vessel; since roots are accustomed to forming underground (in the dark), they don't need light to grow – any watertight cup or pot will work well as a support for the chutes.

Air drying modelling clay
Rolling pin
Cutting tools such as pastry cutters
Greaseproof paper
Cornflour (optional)
Small bowl of water
Acrylic paints
Paintbrushes
Yacht varnish
Glass vessels

1 To soften the clay and make it easy to mould, give it a good knead. Once it feels nice and supple, shape the clay into a smooth ball using the palms of your hands.

Keep any leftover clay re-sealed and in an airtight tub or zip-seal bag to stop it drying out.

2 Their are several ways to create your chute shapes: you can either sculpt and build them by hand, or form them using cutting tools such as pastry cutters or a knife. We prefer to simply manipulate the clay by hand to create a wonky finish.

If you prefer to use cutting tools, roll the ball out on a clean, hard surface lined with greaseproof paper, then cut out the required shape. Cornflour will help to keep the clay from sticking to your work surface or rolling pin.

Regardless of whether you hand-mould or roll-and-cut, make sure the clay isn't too thin, or it may crack as it dries; aim for a minimum of around 5mm (¼ inch) thickness.

If you like, you can create patterns and shape the edges with whichever tools you have to hand.

If you would like to fuse different shapes together, you can make your own clay 'slip' (glue) by mixing a small amount of water with a little lump of clay. Using your scalpel, score the two surfaces that you want to stick together, paint some slip over the grooves and gently press the pieces together.

When you're finished shaping your root chute, make sure to join and smooth any seams – do this by running a wet finger along any cracks and bumps.

3 Leave the chutes to dry for 8 hours, and then return to smooth over any cracks with a wet finger. The clay can still be cut at this point, and can be re-softened with more water if needed.

Leave the chutes to dry completely for another 24 hours, or for as long as indicated on your clay packaging.

4 Once dry, you can decorate the chutes. Gently apply your acrylic paints using a paintbrush. Don't worry if things get a bit messy; just leave the clay to dry in-between coats.

5 Once the final coat of paint has completely dried, use a clean paintbrush to add a layer of varnish to each chute. Make sure to cover the entire surface evenly. After the first layer dries, add another coat of varnish. This will create a protective, watertight finish to prevent the clay going soggy if it sits in water.

Allow the root chutes to dry, then pop them on top of your glass vessels and adorn with your cutting.

Leaf Petiole

Imagine your houseplant as a tree (which indeed it may be), with the central stem being the trunk and the side stems being the branches: the shoot that connects the branch to a leaf is what's known as a petiole.

These young petioles are actively growing from a node – an area that contains a high level of rooting hormones – therefore you will find that petiole cuttings are quick to root and often mature successfully. There are usually many plant petioles to choose from on a healthy plant, so you can propagate any suitable favourites without noticeably changing the overall silhouette of a plant too drastically. Take petiole cuttings in the spring, and by the end of summer you should already notice signs of new growth.

Petioles are often thinner than stems, so sometimes need a bit of extra support while rooting. A toothpick, straw or wooden skewer will make an effective petiole-sized prop, but you can improvise with any rigid material that's not made from metal.

A word of advice: before reaching for your scissors, make sure to flick forward to our propagation table (on pages 98–101) to check your plant is suitable for this method. Certain species (such as the beautifully delicate *Oxalis* and finer-stemmed *Ficus* types) may look like they are the perfect candidates, but sadly can't be successfully propagated in this way, and once cut will quickly wither.

Leaf Petiole Cuttings

Rooting chamber (see p30–35)
  or propagation unit
Compost (see p40)
Rooting boost (see p36–39)
Sharp, sterile knife, scissors or secateurs
Dibber or pencil
Spray mister
Toothpicks, straws or wooden skewers (optional)

The lovely plant we've used on the right is *Peperomia caperata*, which is particularly suited to this technique. Whatever plant you choose, when your leaf petiole cuttings have established new root systems, flick to page 35 to learn about 'hardening off' and 'potting on' – essentially when and how to transplant the cuttings to their new homes.

1 Like stem cuttings, leaf petiole cuttings lose water quickly after being cut. So prepare your rooting chamber and add the rooting compost before taking any cuttings.

2 With a clean spoon, take out a little of your chosen rooting boost (we normally use ground cinnamon for leaf petiole cuttings) and put this aside on a clean surface for later.

3 Remove your cuttings as near to the base of the petiole as possible; aim to leave at least 5cm (2 inches) length of petiole stalk attached. Make one swift cut to avoid crushing delicate petiole material that may not recover. If you don't make a clean cut the first time, trim again just above the first cut until you are satisfied.

4 Dab the cut tip of each petiole stalk in the rooting boost, and gently tap off any excess. Use your dibber or pencil to make a little hole in the rooting compost, then insert the stalk. Gently press some compost around it to secure the stem in place. Repeat this process for each petiole, placing them at least 5cm (2 inches) apart. Prop up any flimsy cuttings with a toothpick, straw or wooden skewer.

5 Finally, seal the cover of your rooting chamber, making sure there are some small holes for ventilation. The cuttings will stay here while they take root, which could take anywhere up from a few weeks.
  Make sure to check on the rooting chamber regularly, spraying the compost only when it feels dry to the touch. Open the bag (or lid) up fully to ventilate the cuttings every few days to prevent mould forming. Remove any affected areas if you see signs of mould growth.

Leaf Vein

We've only recently fallen in love with begonias as houseplants. Ever since Rose was given a cutting from a polka dot Angel Wing (*Begonia coccinea*) belonging to her boyfriend's mum, we've kept our eyes open for other hybrid species to style the vacant spots of our studio. Because begonias prefer indirect sunlight, they can immediately add colour to spots like bookshelves and corner tables. They will flower indoors if you feed them during spring, and are amazingly resilient to pests, too.

There are lots of variations of both flowering and non-flowering types to find at garden centres, and they tend to have wonderfully vibrant leaf shapes and patterns. Look out for *Begonia corallina*, *Begonia rex* and *Begonia metallica*, among others. This method is also a brilliant way to propagate epiphytic orchid cacti (*Epiphyllum*).

The reason these plants make such good candidates for leaf vein cuttings is the distinct veins on their leaves: it is within these veins that the essential rooting elements are stored. One leaf can be carefully sliced into multiple segments – sometimes five or ten – and just a slice of leaf coming into contact with the right compost will trigger root growth.

Like leaf blade and leaf petiole, leaf vein cuttings should be propagated in a rooting chamber (unless you are lucky enough to have a greenhouse). This will help the delicate leaves stay warm and hydrated while they go through the critical rooting phase.

For the best results, propagate from spring to early summer and, as always, make sure to water the parent plant a few days beforehand.

Leaf Vein Cuttings

Rooting chamber (see p30–35)
   or propagation unit
Tropical Houseplant compost (see p40)
Rooting boost, powder (see p36–39)
Sharp, sterile knife
Chopping board
Fine, coated wire
Spray mister

To help demonstrate the variations this technique encompasses, we've used different plants in the photos opposite. At the top (and on page 80) is painted leaf begonia (*Begonia rex*), and below is cape primrose (*Streptocarpus*).

1 Before you begin cutting, prepare your rooting chamber and add the rooting compost before taking any cuttings. It's also sensible to prepare your rooting boost, to avoid the cuttings hanging around. With a clean spoon, take out a little of your chosen rooting boost and put this aside on a clean surface for later.

2 Use a knife or scissors to remove the leaf. Lay it on a chopping board. Cut the petiole (stalk) off so that you can lay the leaf down flat. Use your knife to slice the leaf into postage-stamp-sized pieces, each containing at least one section of primary vein (the main vein that runs down the leaf).

Alternatively, you can cut the leaf into as many larger pieces as you like – it's up to you and how many new plants you wish to propagate.

You can, if you like, keep the leaf whole, and make small, perpendicular cuts along the most prominent veins of the leaf.

Essentially, any cut vein that touches the rooting compost should spring into rooting action.

3 Gently dab your rooting boost along any cut edges that bisect a vein. You will need a minimal amount of powder for this; only the very edge should be coated.

Next, lay each leaf piece on the surface of the rooting compost a couple of centimetres (about 1 inch) apart.

4 Cut some short lengths of wire and curve them into U shapes. Then anchor the leaf parts down by piercing through them and into the compost, being careful to avoid the veins. Pinning the leaf parts in this way will prevent tiny, delicate roots being disturbed as they first start to develop.

To ensure root growth, make sure the leaf veins are either directly touching (or even slightly buried beneath) the rooting compost.

5 Close the cover of your rooting chamber, and make sure there are some holes for ventilation. The cuttings will take root over the next few months depending on the conditions – plenty of natural light (or grow lights) can really speed the process up.

6 Monitor the moisture level of the rooting chamber compost regularly. Carefully spritz the surface (avoiding directly spraying the cut leaves) only when the compost feels dry to the touch. Keep in mind that too much moisture will cause rot to form. Open the chamber bag (or lid) fully to ventilate the cuttings every few days to prevent mould forming. If mould does form, pick out and discard any affected areas quickly.

For details on how to transplant newly rooting leaves, see page 35.

Succulent Leaves

Amazingly, succulents have adapted to multiply with no help at all. They often shed their juicy leaves to conserve energy, and each healthy leaf contains enough hormones to root without having to be buried. The process takes quite a bit longer than succulent stem cuttings (page 62), but couldn't be more straightforward. With just a shallow tray and some rooting compost, you have the potential to grow ten or twenty babies from a single succulent plant.

This makes sharing certain succulents really easy; if you discover an exotic plant at a friend's house or on your travels, you can simply tweak off a few leaves without affecting the look of the original plant much at all. A matchbox or small pot makes a good case to protect the leaves from getting squashed in your bag. Don't keep them in the dark for longer than a few days, though.

Not all succulents will reproduce in this way, but there are hundreds of species which happily will: those from the *Sedum, Crassula, Echeveria, Kalanchoe* and *Rhipsalis* genera are a great place to start.

Many succulents also produce offsets or suckers, which are miniature clones that appear below the soil level and can also easily be separated. You can find out more about these on pages 128–133.

Succulent Leaf Cuttings

Sharp, sterile knife, scissors or secateurs (optional)
Pots or trays with drainage trays
Cacti & Other Succulents compost (p40)
Spray mister or watering can

It's really important to water the succulent a day or so beforehand. This is because, once removed, the leaf will rely solely on its store of moisture to develop new roots, which might take a few months.

The photographs show variations of the technique using a few plants: top left is Mexican giant (*Echeveria colorata*); top right are assorted *Echeveria*; at the bottom is orchid cactus (*Epiphyllum*).

1 Select some leaves from the middle of the stem – these are likely to be fairly mature but still young enough to have plenty of rooting power. You may need to remove some of the lower leaves to get to those higher up.

2 To remove them, gently pinch each leaf between your thumb and index finger as close to the stem as possible. Carefully tweak the leaf back and forwards, up and down until it comes loose, taking care not to rip it. It is essential for the leaf to come away cleanly at the very point that it connects to the stem, because this is the only spot that roots can shoot from. If easier, you can use a sharp, sterile knife for this step.

If possible, choose quite a few leaves – ten or more – as not all leaves will produce healthy roots, and even those that do may not survive long-term. It's best to overcompensate to make sure you are left with plenty of strong babies.

3 Lay the leaves on a dry, clean surface and leave them indoors somewhere fairly bright but out of direct sunlight. This is so that the leaves don't dry out while the ends callous over. After a minimum of three days, they are ready to be planted.

4 To prepare your rooting pot or tray, give it a good clean and fill it with a layer of compost. Spray the surface with water to dampen it slightly.

If you are propagating *Echeveria*, simply lay the leaves on the surface of the compost, where they will naturally take root without being buried.
For other succulents, stick the calloused leaf ends into the compost just deep enough for them to stand unsupported.

Keep the tray somewhere warm and bright. Over the following weeks, keep the soil moist but never wet.

5 After some weeks or months, depending on the season, you will spy the first, tiny signs of growing roots, and often a miniature rosette of leaves. At this point you can cover the roots with a little compost to encourage more growth. Don't be tempted to remove the original succulent leaf, as it will still be acting as a reserve of water and nutrients for the tiny plantlet.

6 A while later, when the babies are more developed, you can carefully transplant them to new, individual pots using a small spoon as a shovel. Keep the baby succulents somewhere bright and continue to care for them as you would your other succulents. From now on, it is best to water them from below using a drainage tray. After six months or so, you will notice the original leaf either drop off naturally or dry up and wither, at which point it can be safely removed or simply buried under more compost.

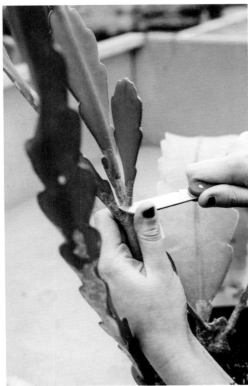

Leaf Blade

For plants that don't have obvious petioles or stems, and no central vein, leaf blade cuttings are the solution. It's also good to employ this technique when you would like to produce multiple plantlets from one leaf. Even though it's not a method that's suitable for many popular houseplants, for those it does suit, the results are really satisfying; like the leaf vein technique on page 78, we find it magical to watch how these part-leaf cuttings regenerate themselves.

Because you only need a single leaf to experiment with, leaf blade cuttings are ideal if you have a favourite plant that you want to propagate, but would like to avoid altering its appearance too much; you can take a single leaf discreetly from the back and turn it into lots of healthy babies. For example, with just one slender leaf from a snake plant or a *Eucomis*, you can easily produce five or ten viable cuttings. The key is that these leaves are particularly fleshy, so each slice has a reserve of moisture to keep it alive while it tries to take root. Even so, using a rooting chamber is essential to prevent the cuttings drying out.

Leaf Blade Cuttings

Rooting chamber (see p30–35)
    or propagation unit
Compost (see p40)
Sharp, sterile knife and chopping board, or scissors
Marker pen
Spray mister

For the best results, propagate leaf blade cuttings from spring to early summer, and remember to water the plant a few days beforehand. The example on these pages uses the snake plant, which is an ideal leaf blade candidate. But do note that the sap of the plant can be moderately toxic to humans and animals if eaten, so make sure to wash your hands after handling and keep plants safely out of reach of any curious hands or paws.

1 Start by setting up your rooting chamber. Once the compost is in place, pre-moisten it before moving on to the next step – it should be moist throughout, but not soggy.

2 With one clean cut, remove a whole leaf, slicing as close to the base as you can. Lay the leaf down on the chopping board. The next step is to cut the leaf into horizontal sections, allowing each portion to measure around 7–10cm (3–4 inches) in length. Only the lower cut of each leaf cutting can root, so during this step you might find it handy to mark the end with your pen so you don't get mixed up.

3 Use your knife to carve some channels in the compost to a depth of 3–5cm (1½–2 inches). This will reduce tissue damage to your cuttings when you press them in place. Push each cut end into the compost, pressing them in to secure them.

4 Partially cover your rooting chamber, and allow space for ventilation, which will prevent a build-up of moisture.
   Monitor the moisture level of the compost over the next few months, spraying the surface only when it feels dry to the touch. A build-up of moisture can cause mould, so make sure to open the lid (or bag) up fully every couple of days to ventilate the cuttings. If you notice any mould, remove any affected areas as soon as possible to prevent it spreading.

5 After two to three months, you should notice little trumpet-shaped shoots sprouting next to each successful cutting. Once these shoots are around 10cm (4 inches) tall, flick to page 35 to learn how to repot your plantlets.

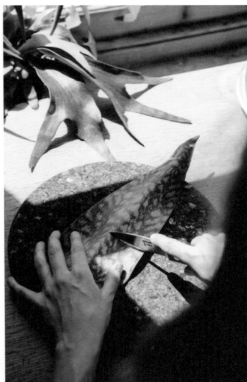

Indoor Plant Propagation Table

O n the following pages, we have created a propagation table that features some common genera, such as *Agave* and *Philodendron*, which in reality include many individual species. The suggested propagation methods given will most likely apply to all the houseplants in that genus, but you might like to double-check the method is suitable for your particular species of plant first.

To help you have as much possible success, we have included the ideal timings to propagate each plant. Because many houseplants enter a dormant phase during autumn and winter, asexual propagation is best carried out in the spring and summer, when they are active and strong. However, if you keep your houseplants warm all year round, they may stay active all year. Look for new shoots or flowers as signs of growth, indicating the plant can be propagated confidently.

Many houseplants such as palms and cacti can also be grown sexually with seeds; if you would like to experiment we suggest doing a little research first, and source the right equipment, to give you the best chance of success.

Adiantum raddianum **Maidenhair fern**	Divide / Spring
Aechmea fasciata **Urn plant bromeliad**	Remove offsets / Late spring or early summer
Aeonium	Stem or leaf petiole cuttings / Spring
Agave	Remove offsets / Spring or summer
Aglaonema **Chinese evergreen**	Stem cuttings, air layer or divide / Spring
Alocasia	Remove offsets / Spring
Aloe	Stem cuttings or remove offsets / Late spring or early summer
Asparagus setaceus **Asparagus fern**	Divide / Early spring
Aspidistra **Cast iron plant**	Divide / Spring
Begonia (Cane-stemmed)	Stem, leaf petiole or leaf vein cuttings / Spring or summer
Begonia (Rhizomatous)	Divide rhizomes / Spring or summer
Caladium **Elephant ear**	Remove offsets / Spring
Calathea	Divide plants / Late spring or early summer
Ceropegia woodii **String of hearts**	Stem cuttings / Late spring or early summer
Chamaedorea costaricana **Bamboo palm**	Remove offsets / Late spring or early summer
Chamaedorea elegans **Parlour palm**	Remove offsets / Late spring or early summer
Chlorophytum comosum **Spider plant**	Divide / Early spring to late autumn / Plant runners all year round
Citrus	Stem cuttings / Late spring or summer

Cleistocactus coladmononis **Monkey's tail cactus**	Remove offsets / Spring or summer
Clivia	Divide / Late winter or early spring
Codiaeum **Croton**	Stem cuttings / Summer Air layer / Spring
Crassula	Stem or leaf cuttings / Spring or summer
Cycas revoluta **Sago palm**	Remove offsets / Late spring or early summer
Cylindropuntia bigelovii **Teddy bear cactus**	Remove offsets / Spring or summer
Dieffenbachia **Dumb cane**	Stem cuttings or air layer / Spring or summer
Dischidia ruscifolia **Million hearts**	Succulent stem cuttings / Spring or early summer
Dracaena	Stem cuttings or air layer / Spring or summer
Dypsis lutescens **Areca palm**	Remove offsets / Late spring or early summer
Echeveria	Stem or leaf cuttings or remove offsets / Spring or summer
Epiphyllum **Orchid cactus**	Leaf or leaf vein cuttings / Spring or summer
Epipremnum aureum **Golden pothos**	Stem cuttings or ground layer / Spring or summer
Eucomis **Pineapple plant**	Leaf blade cuttings / Early to mid-summer
Euphorbia tirucalli **Pencil cactus**	Stem cuttings / Spring or summer (use gloves to avoid irritation from sap)
Ficus benjamina **Weeping fig**	Stem cuttings or air layer / Spring
Ficus elastica **Rubber plant**	Stem cuttings or air layer / Spring or summer
Ficus lyrata **Fiddle-leaf fig**	Stem cuttings or air layer / Spring or summer

Haworthia	Remove offsets / Spring or summer
Hedera helix English ivy	Stem cuttings or ground layer / Spring or summer
Howea belmoreana Belmore sentry palm	Remove offsets / Late spring or early summer
Howea forsteriana Kentia palm	Remove offsets / Late spring or early summer
Hoya Wax plant	Stem cuttings or ground layer / Spring or summer
Kalanchoe laetivirens Mother of thousands	Root plantlets / All year round
Kalanchoe thyrsiflora Paddle plant	Leaf cuttings / Spring or summer
Maranta leuconera Prayer plant	Divide or take stem cuttings / Spring
Monstera deliciosa Swiss cheese plant	Stem cuttings / Summer Air layer / Autumn
Musa basjoo Banana palm	Remove offsets or divide / Late spring or early summer, every five years
Nephrolepis exaltata Boston fern	Divide / Spring or summer Separate rooted runners / Early spring
Oxalis triangularis	Divide / Spring or summer
Peperomia	Remove offsets or stem or leaf petiole cuttings / Spring or summer
Persea americana Avocado	Stem cuttings / Spring or summer
Philodendron	Stem or leaf petiole cuttings, or ground layer / Spring or summer
Pilea cadierei Aluminium plant	Stem cuttings / Spring or summer
Pilea peperomioides Chinese money plant	Remove offsets or stem or leaf petiole cuttings / Spring or summer
Rhipsalis	Leaf or stem cuttings / Spring or summer

Rhoicissus	Stem or leaf petiole cuttings / Spring or summer
Saintpaulia **African violet**	Leaf petiole cuttings / Spring or summer
Sansevieria **Snake plant**	Remove offsets, divide or leaf blade cuttings / Spring
Saxifraga stolonifera **Strawberry begonia**	Divide or root runners / All year round
Schefflera	Stem cuttings or air layer / Spring
Schlumbergera **Christmas cactus**	Divide or stem cuttings / Spring or summer
Sedum morganianum **Burro's tail/donkey tail**	Stem or leaf cuttings / Spring or summer
Sempervivum	Divide, remove offsets or leaf cuttings / Spring or summer
Senecio rowleyanus **String of beads**	Stem cuttings / Spring or summer
Spathiphyllum **Peace lily**	Divide / Autumn or after flowering
Strelitzia **Bird of paradise flower**	Remove offsets or divide / Late spring or early summer
Syngonium podophyllum **Arrowhead vine**	Divide or take stem cuttings / Spring or summer
Tillandsia **Air plants**	Generally, remove offsets when they are at least one third the size of the parent plant
Tradescantia **Wandering Jew**	Stem cuttings / All year round
Vriesea splendens **Flaming sword**	Remove offsets / Spring or summer
Yucca	Divide, remove offsets or take stem cuttings / Spring or summer
Zamioculcas zamiifolia **ZZ plant**	Divide or take stem cuttings / Spring or summer

Division & Grafting

There must be some alchemy in those leaves where a place exists, of late summer skies, wet grass, beautiful voices and cold hands

Lindsay Sekulowicz, The Plant

Division

During the making of our first book, *House of Plants*,
Rose and I both became attached to an asparagus fern,
which doubled in size soon after we bought it (I quickly
snuck it into my bedroom). It generally brightened any
space (but mainly my bedroom) that we styled it in.
When it came to Rose moving out, we were faced with
a problem: who would get to keep it?

Fortunately, we didn't have to decide: our favourite
plant was easy to share, simply by cutting it straight
down the middle.

Houseplants that are suitable for splitting into entire
sections are those that grow in clusters rather than one
central point, such as most succulents, *Calathea* and
the popular peace lily. Division also works well for plants
that produce rhizomes, such as ferns, snake plant,
orchids and the ZZ plant.

By separating off a portion of the plant which already
includes all the crucial elements – roots, stems and
leaves – you will not only instantly produce brand new,
impressive plants, you will also encourage healthy
growth all round, avoiding the overcrowding of roots
which will eventually occur in any lively potted plant.

Other than repotting, division is the best way to save
a mature plant which might become pot-bound. Look
out for external signs of overcrowding, such as roots
coming through the pot's drainage holes, diminishing
health or, if plastic, a bulging pot.

The best time to divide a plant is from early spring
to late summer, or whenever it is actively growing.
This will ensure its roots and stems are at their most
resilient and able to withstand the abrupt shock of
being interfered with.

Division Method

Sheet or table cloth
Pots with drainage holes and trays
Drainage stones
Compost (see p40)
Sharp knife
Topdressing stones (optional)

Before you begin, have a closer look at the base of the stems to determine the root structure and ideal cutting points. Next, decide how drastically you would like to reduce the size of the parent plant and how many new plants you wish to produce. This will determine the quantities of the materials you will need.

Unlike other methods, it's better not to water the plant beforehand, as this can make the compost much more tricky to separate.

This method is suited to many houseplants, but not all. Here we're using an asparagus fern. But you should check the propagation table on pages 98–101 before dividing your plant.

1 Lay a large sheet or tablecloth down to catch any rogue soil. Prepare your new pot by putting a layer of drainage stones at the base and adding a good handful or two of compost.

2 To remove a thinner-stemmed plant from its pot, rest the palm of your hand flat along the surface of the soil, fingers spread out to support the stems. Then gently turn the pot upside down. If the plant doesn't budge, you may need to loosen the soil around the edges of the pot with a pencil or knife first.

Large, thick-stemmed plants can be removed by carefully lifting from the base of the stems. Never pull too hard; if the plant seems stuck then check for any roots that may have knotted around the drainage holes and may need pruning off. Give the plastic pot a squeeze to help release the plant. If none of these methods work, you may need to cut the plastic pot away.

3 Once removed, carefully sit the plant back down, either upright or on its side depending on how rigid the compost is, making sure not to crush any more fragile stems if you lay it on its side.

4 Using a sharp knife, locate the first point at which you would like to divide the plant and slice straight down in between the stems and roots. Repeat until you have created as many new divisions as you want. A very sharp knife will ensure you get a clean cut and prevent badly damaging the roots. But don't worry about slicing through roots, as they will regenerate themselves in no time.

5 Replant each of the divided sections in their new pots, replacing any lost compost from the parent plant's pot too. Pack the compost down gently, enough to support the plant but not so solid that it suffocates the roots and makes watering impossible. If you would like to top-dress the plant with stones – which can help to prevent flies laying eggs in the compost – remember to leave enough space in the pot.

6 Finally, choose a position for each new plant that suits the parent plant's lighting and temperature requirements. If any of the plants wilt, encase them within a clear plastic bag to give them a boost of humidity. Once they perk up, you can gradually open the bag up to help the plant acclimatise, eventually removing it.

Grafting

This is a technique usually associated with fruit trees such as cherry and apple, to optimise the characteristics of different species. For example, in order to produce a harvest of fruit at the perfect picking height, the upper portion of a particularly delicious cherry tree might be grafted (fused) with the stump of another type that won't grow too tall.

Indoors, cacti can be grafted together purely for fun. Or perhaps a favourite cactus has an ailment and might not survive without propagating a healthy chunk from it – this can then be grafted to another. For us, it is mainly a creative way to experiment with bizarre silhouettes that add a bit of joy to the sunniest spots of our homes.

The upper part of the graft (chosen for its stems) is called the scion, and the lower (chosen for its roots) is called the rootstock. Generally, grafting is most successful when the scion and the rootstock are genetically alike, but with hardy cacti it's possible to fuse two wildly varying cacti, even sometimes from different genera, that you love the look of in order to create a totally unique hybrid.

You can get to grips with the technique by trying it out on commonly used species. For the rootstock, try those found within the *Lemaireocereus*, *Trichocereus*, *Cereus*, *Hylocereus* and *Opuntia* genera. For the scion, look out for species of *Sulcorebutia*, *Echinomastus*, *Lophophora* and *Strombocactus*, among many others.

Always graft in the spring or early summer when cacti are growing vigorously. This will give both the scion and the rootstock the best chance of healing together and surviving long-term.

One final thought: what with the fairly brutal nature of grafting techniques, inevitably some plants won't survive, so we recommend having fun with cacti you're not too precious about and can be more carefree with.

Grafting Method

Sharp, sterile scalpel or grafting knife
Pure rubbing alcohol and clean cloth
Leather gardening gloves (optional)
Elastic bands

Three or four days before you begin your graft, water the cacti so that they are as healthy as possible. It is equally important to make sure excess water is allowed to drain away, as you do not want the plant to be waterlogged when you cut into it. The cacti we've chosen to graft are two species from the *Cereus* and *Echinopsis* genera – and both were in great health. If either cacti look dry or unhealthy inside when cut, they are not viable and should be discarded.

1 To begin grafting, clean the surface you are working on and disinfect your knife by rubbing it with a little alcohol. Check your knife is very sharp, so that you can make neat cuts and minimise tissue damage.

2 Try not to prolong the following steps to avoid the scion or rootstock drying out. Put on your gloves to protect your fingers from spines and make the first cut to the rootstock, slicing the top portion cleanly away with at least 4cm (2 inches) of height left at the base. If you like, you can save the top half by treating it as an offset (see pages 128–133).

3 Next, bevel the edges of the rootstock with angled cuts. This will make aligning the scion easier. After all edges of the rootstock are bevelled, make one final cut to its top to ensure the surface is as moist as possible for the next step.

4 Take your second scion cactus and slice off the portion you wish to graft, making the cut as flat and even as possible. Look out for a ring of tissue – called the 'vascular cambium' – on the cut surface. These rings mark the source of new growth within each plant and are crucial for successful grafting.

5 The next step is to align the rootstock and the scion. It's crucial to make sure that the cut surfaces are flat and positioned together so that even some small parts of the vascular cambium rings are overlapping. This may mean you have to align the cacti off-centre, but there will be a very slim chance of the graft fusing successfully otherwise.

6 Once the two pieces are in position, fix with a couple of elastic bands looped over the top of the scion and around the base of the pot. You want the pressure to be tight enough that the cut surfaces are pressed together securely, but not so tight that the scion is damaged. Try to position the elastic bands in a straight cross so that the connection doesn't shift over time.

Applying firm pressure and aligning the cut edges precisely allows water, minerals and other nutrients to pass from the rootstock plant to the scion, while sealing out rogue bacteria. This will give the graft the best chance of forming a strong and long-lasting connection.

7 While it heals, leave the grafted plant in a spot away from direct light and at a comfortable room temperature. When the soil dries out completely, water from below using a drainage tray.

8 After a couple of months, remove the rubber bands; you should find that the plants have fused together. From now on you can start to care for it as you would your other cacti.

SELF-WATERING POT

Most of the prettiest planters on the market have a major disadvantage: they don't have drainage holes. Unsurprisingly, when we visit our friends' houses and are asked for advice on ailing plants, they are almost always those that are housed within a sealed pot. Without a way for excess water to escape, these plants will inevitably suffer from the growth of bacteria and eventually root damage.

Unfortunately, shop-bought self-watering pots tend to be either very ugly, very expensive, or both.

This self-watering pot design is suitable for any indoor tropical plant that likes its soil to be moist – but not soaking – at all times. If you're not sure, generally these are plants native to more humid climates, such as ferns, palms, *Alocasia* and the majestic peace lily. The built-in reservoir is also a brilliant solution if you travel and have to leave your more fussy indoor plants unattended for a while.

Tropical plant in its original plastic pot (this will be your inner pot)
Planter (around 1½–2 times the volume of the inner pot)
Porous fabric such as cotton or a clean tea towel – anything that
    will soak up water effectively
Scissors
A handful of activated charcoal
Bag of aqua clay pebbles
Cup
Fine topdressing stones (optional)

1 Give the materials a good clean to remove any potentially harmful bacteria. Wash the pots with soap and water; thoroughly rinse the drainage and topdressing stones and – unless it is brand new – run the fabric through your washing machine. If using, there is no need to clean the activated charcoal.

2 When you're ready, remove the plant from its plastic pot: support the base of the stems with the palm of your hand and turn the pot upside down. If the plant stays put, you may need to prune off any rogue roots growing through the drainage holes. Once removed, lay the plant gently on its side ensuring you don't crush any stems. You can use some scrunched up newspaper to help prop up the stem.

3 Cut strips of fabric to a length of around three times the height of your larger planter. Make sure to cut each strip to a width that will allow it to be threaded through a drainage hole of your inner pot. You will need half the number of strips to the number of drainage holes. For example, if your inner pot has six holes, you will need three strips of fabric.

4 Thread each strip of fabric through one drainage hole and then back down another, pulling until it is taut. You should be left with the two halves of the strip hanging down below the pot. Repeat this until all of the strips are threaded.

5 Sprinkle the activated charcoal into the base of the larger planter, and then add the aqua clay pebbles on top. You want to fill the planter so that the inner pot can rest on top of the pebbles with its rim a couple of centimetres (about an inch) below the lip of the planter.

6 This step is a little fiddly: the idea is to get the strips of fabric to nestle in among the stones all the way down to the base of the planter. This is so that water can soak the fabric and travel up the strips all the way to the soil line.

7 Once the plastic pot and fabric strips are securely embedded, you can replace the plant in its original plastic pot where it will sit on top of the fabric strips. Using your cup, fill the pebble reservoir with water until it just reaches the top of the clay pebbles. Make a note of how many cups it takes to do this.

8 Fill in the space around the plastic pot with more aqua clay pebbles and then top-dress until the pot is concealed.
    Over the next few hours, as your pot starts its magic, you should find that the top of the compost becomes damp to the touch.
    Later on, you will know when it is time to top up the water reservoir by simply checking the dampness of the compost with your finger. As soon as it feels bone dry, you know it's time to top up the reservoir.

Runners, Offsets & Suckers

There are flowers everywhere
for those who want to see them

Henri Matisse

Runners

When it comes to runners, two indoor plants immediately spring to mind: the tough-as-nails spider plant and the lily-pad-shaped strawberry begonia – both regularly throw out miniature plantlets that contain all of the necessary material to grow independently. All they need is a bit of soil.

To be a bit more exact, a runner is actually a modified stem that has adapted to be more flexible, shooting itself out horizontally with the hope of reaching the ground. The runner acts as a source of nutrients and water, and therefore new root growth, sometimes even before meeting soil – often you will see a runner that has already begun to grow roots in the air.

In the wild, these runners would hope to naturally meet the ground, take root and slowly blossom into fully-grown specimens. Of course, when potted up indoors and left to dangle beyond the edge of the pot, the baby plants normally fan out in a beautiful (but slightly aimless) arrangement until they eventually dry up and wither.

We like to think of the runners as the next generation of a plant; if you're willing to give a helping hand, you can make the most of every single one, and each can go on to mature and throw out its own babies later down the line.

Once rooted they make brilliant gifts for loved ones – all the more special having come direct from a plant you have nurtured.

Runners Method

Small pots with drainage holes
Tropical Houseplant compost (see p40)
Drainage trays
Small drainage stones
A few hairpins
Scissors

Try to pick runners which look hydrated and strong, with signs of healthy growth. You can choose to plant lots or a few runners at a time, but we recommend putting your efforts into only the healthiest runners to prevent disappointment later down the line. Here we've planted up five or six from the parent spider plant.

Keep in mind that the runners will still be attached to the parent plant and won't want to be disturbed while initially setting down roots, so choose a spot in your home you are happy to give up for a few months.

By leaving the runner attached to the parent plant, water and nutrients can still be delivered to the baby plantlet, which will grow its own root system much more quickly with this extra nourishment. That said, if a plantlet becomes detached from the stem before it has developed roots, you can still continue with the propagation, it will just take a little while longer.

1 Prepare the pots and drainage trays by cleaning them thoroughly and filling with compost. Press the compost down gently so that there are no big air pockets. Water the compost so that it is moist throughout. Allow any excess moisture to drain away. Fill the drainage trays with a shallow layer of drainage stones.

2 Identify the runners on the parent plant and make sure the attached stem of each runner isn't pulled too tight. Then stretch each runner on its stem from the parent plant towards its new pot.

3 Before planting the runner, have a look to see if there are already roots growing. If so, you might need to make a dip in the compost with your finger.

If you have a cluster of plantlets on one runner, all the better – you can separate them later on once they have developed roots.

4 Take a hairpin and stretch it out a little so that its grip loosens slightly. Use this as a peg to anchor the runner firmly into the compost.

5 Check the parent and baby plants' compost regularly to ensure it stays moist in both pots, but not drenched. The layer of stones within the drainage tray will help to increase humidity and keep the new plantlet from drying out in between watering.

6 After a couple of months, you can check if roots have formed by carefully removing the hairpin and giving the baby plant a very gentle pull upwards. If you feel resistance, you know that a root system has formed. If the plant starts to come away from the compost, leave it alone and check again in another month.

Once the baby plants have fully rooted, the connected runner stem can be removed – trim it with sharp scissors as close to the parent plant and new plant as possible.

Offsets & Suckers

Last summer, while visiting her boyfriend's family in Cyprus, a relative invited Rose to explore her ancient succulent garden. She led her between rows of low walls, where a diverse landscape of teddy bear cacti, sedums and climbing *Rhipsalis* had been carefully created over the years, many of them contributions from her dearest friends and family members. Rose returned home to Margate with bottles full of the most unusual cacti cuttings, each with its own history.

Meanwhile, back in London, my good friends Camille and Salomé were visiting from Paris. Before they left, they carefully took offsets from some of my rarest cacti and succulents, leaving with a tissue-lined plastic box containing prickly fragments to be transplanted to their apartment.

Miraculously, almost all of the offsets survived once in their new homes, and we realised just how fruitful it can be to collect succulents while travelling.

The trick is that, unlike the stem cuttings of more tropical species, the raw ends of cacti and succulent offsets should be left to callous over after they are separated from the parent plant. This means that both the offset and its story are easily transported from one home to another, without the need for compost.

Offsets (called suckers if they are growing from the roots of the plant) are miniature clones that naturally emerge either from the main stem or below the soil line, often after the plant has flowered. They are found on desert cacti, *Agaves*, *Aloe* and bromeliads, but also on palms and the snake plant.

Like cuttings, offsets can also be taken as a last resort when a plant is suffering from a pest infestation, using the healthy portions to regenerate the life of the original plant as if by magic.

Offsets With Roots

Sharp, sterile knife
Tropical Houseplant compost (see p40)
Plant pots and drainage trays
Small drainage stones
Watering can or spray mister
Clear plastic bag (optional)

It's important to identify whether the offset already has roots. Offsets that grow around or just below the soil line of the plant often already do, especially for tropical plants such as *Peperomia*, snake plant, palms and bromeliads. Here we're using a urn plant bromeliad (*Aechmea fasciata*).

When it comes to desert cacti (which tend to be the standing, prickly sort) offsets are often seen growing higher up the stem. One familiar example is the bunny ears cactus (*Opuntia microdasys*), whose 'ears' are actually offsets. In this case, rooting will be much slower, but very straightforward, using the method for offsets without roots on page 133.

Before taking an offset from a succulent or a tropical plant, ideally let it mature to at least a third of the size of the parent plant. This will give it the best chance of surviving independently. It is best to propagate with this method in the spring or early summer, giving the new plant the best chance of rooting.

1 To prepare your materials, line your drainage tray with a layer of small stones, and fill your pot with fresh compost. Dampen the surface of the compost with a little water, just enough so that it is moist to touch.

2 Gently take the entire plant out of its pot. Begin to remove some of the compost around the offset with your fingers to determine how large the root system is. Continue to tease away as much old compost neighbouring the offset as possible, so that you can identify where best to cut, but don't worry if you have to leave some compost intact.

3 Avoid damaging the roots as much as possible: use your knife to slice through the material connecting the offset to the parent plant. Replace the parent plant in its original pot.

4 Make a dip with your fingers in the fresh compost, keeping in mind that you will ideally pot the offset and its root system at the same depth at which it was originally growing. If the offset is larger than you imagined, simply set it aside until you have prepared a larger pot.

5 Place the offset into the dip you made, burying the roots with compost and pressing down gently. Make sure the roots and offset base are covered and the new plant is anchored so that it stands securely by itself.

Sit the pot on its drainage tray and water the plant very gently around the inner edges of the pot, allowing any excess moisture to sit among the drainage stones for humidity.

6 Finally, you can fill in any spaces left in the parent plant's compost, which will give it a little boost of nutrients and ensure it is safely supported for future growth. If either parent or baby plant wilts or shows signs of dehydration, you can encase it inside the clear plastic bag to increase humidity while it acclimatises/recovers.

Offsets Without Roots

Leather gloves or scrunched up newspaper (optional)
Sharp, sterile knife or scalpel
Rooting boost, ground cinnamon (see p36–39), optional
Plant pot and drainage tray
Handful of small drainage stones
Cacti & Other Succulents compost (see p40)
Spray mister

The photographs here show *Opuntia consolea* and its offsets; this method is ideal for desert cacti offsets, which are often seen growing off the main stem. But many air plants also produce rootless offsets, or 'pups' at the base of their leaves. If you would like to remove a pup to grow independently, wait until it is at least a third of the size of the parent plant, then give both the parent plant and offset a generous soaking in room temperature water. You should then be able to gently separate it with your fingers.

1 If you are removing a spiky cactus offset, you can use gloves or scrunched up newspaper to protect your fingers and support the offset while you cut. Use your knife to make a clean cut at the base of the offset. Plants often self-propagate by producing offsets, so you may find that they come away without too much effort.

2 Cacti and succulent offsets with no roots should be left for a few days before planting. This allows the cut end to dry out and callous, reducing the chance of harmful bacteria growing. If you like, you can first dust the cut end with a pinch of ground cinnamon rooting boost, and then place the offset somewhere cool, bright and away from direct sunlight.

If you are taking the offset while away from home, the ground cinnamon is not essential, and the offset can be carefully transported in an airtight container until you are ready to plant it. As long as you can give it some indirect light, the offset should survive unplanted for at least a week or two.

3 After three or four days, the cut end should have calloused over. Prepare your pot: line the drainage tray with small stones, fill the pot with fresh compost, and spray the surface with a little water to dampen. Then simply bury the cut end in the compost, deep enough that the offset is supported upright.

4 Leave the offset somewhere with plenty of bright, indirect light while it roots, misting the compost a little only when it feels completely dry to the touch.

Rooting may take up to six months. You will be able to tell whether roots have formed by very gently pulling the offset. If you feel resistance, you know the offset has rooted. If you feel any signs of movement, replace the offset to give it longer to root. If you wish to repot it, we recommend leaving the plantlet undisturbed for at least a year to develop.

Runners, Offsets & Suckers

Layering

We shall not cease from exploration
And the end of all our exploring
Will be to arrive where we started
And know the place for the first time

T.S Eliot

O ne of the oldest methods of propagation, layering is thought to have been first practised in ancient times by Chinese bonsai growers. Like taking cuttings, the process creates an exact replica (genetically, at least) of the parent plant, because it uses existing plant material.

There are two techniques: ground layering and air layering. With both, the idea is to help a plant produce a new root system along one of its branches while part of this branch remains attached to the parent plant. This is achieved by slicing away part of the outer layer of the branch while leaving the inner core (containing the essential tissue which is capable of new root growth) intact. By introducing this inner plant tissue to the right rooting medium, a whole new system of roots can form. Once this happens, the branch and its newly grown roots can be removed, and this replica plant can sustain itself independently.

Because the inner material of the branch remains attached during root development, the parent plant provides support, water and nutrients to the area of new root growth, helping it to become strong and protecting it from damage or disease. This also means that, unlike some other methods of propagation, layering doesn't require such special control of temperature and humidity, making the technique much less technically challenging overall.

The difference between ground and air layering is that ground layering encourages the stem down to the ground to root, while air layering involves bringing the rooting compost up to the stem. It follows that air layering is most suitable for thicker-stemmed plants that have less flexible stems.

Don't be put off by having to make precise cuts – it's really not as technical as it sounds, and the whole thing will give you such a sense of achievement when, after a month or so, you see healthy new roots starting to grow and you have the satisfaction of multiplying some of your favourite, large indoor plants in a relatively short space of time.

You can try layering at any time of year, providing your home is warm and blessed with year-round natural light. Indoor plants that are kept in darker, colder conditions during winter months will likely become dormant and probably won't respond positively to this method until the start of spring.

Air Layering

There are two favourite houseplants that people are always keen to learn how to propagate: the rubber plant and the fiddle-leaf fig. Larger, woody species of house plants like these two don't always respond well to cuttings, because their roots grow very slowly and they are therefore much more susceptible to disease or damage at the vulnerable stage of root development. Other suitable plants include *Aglaonema*, *Croton* and *Dieffenbachia*.

We first discovered air layering through one of my most treasured plants, an elderly *Dracaena marginata*, fondly named Marge, which I inherited from my beloved grandmother. More than 40 years old, Marge's spindly stems would have sudden growth spurts each spring, gradually outgrowing each new spot I manoeuvred her into. I eventually needed a stepladder to reach her tallest stems, which were by that point tickling the ceiling and showing no sign of slowing down, despite my desperate pleas for her to travel in any direction but up.

Air layering is ideal for reviving older, thicker-stemmed plants like Marge that have lost some of their foliage and become 'leggy', or have simply outgrown the space you have styled for them in your home. If the stems of the plant are softer and easily bent downwards, ground layering (see pages 145–147) may be the more suitable method to experiment with.

As explained previously, air layering involves bringing the rooting medium up to a branch. This aerial action is brilliant for those living in smaller urban spaces since it allows the parent plant to be kept in its original spot, and doesn't require lots of extra pots or space to nurture the new plant growth.

Air Layering Method

Sphagnum moss (available from garden centres)
Small bowl or cup of tepid water
Sharp, sterile knife or scalpel
Rooting boost, powder (see p36–39)
Plastic wrapping material (an A4 plastic sleeve works well)
Some string, wire or bin bag ties
Toothpick or match (optional)
Pipette, jug or spoon
A while later: pots and compost (see p40)

Before you reach for your knife, we recommend carefully reading through all of the steps first. There are a couple of slightly fiddly points and you may appreciate a hand from someone else, particularly if the plant you are propagating is very tall. The plant being used in the step-by-step photographs is strangler fig (*Ficus aurea*).

1 Begin by preparing the sphagnum moss – soak a generous handful in a cup or bowl of tepid water.

2 Next, look at your plant for a mature stem that is quite rigid – no thinner than a pencil – with a woody appearance. Remember that once the new root mass has developed, you will be removing the entire stem from the parent plant, so you will want to pick a stem you are happy to eventually prune off entirely. Trim off leaves and sideshoots from the area you are going to cut.

Identify where you will make the cut: this should be at a point 30–60cm (12–24 inches) below the top sprout of leaves, just below a node (the point on the where side stems grow). This is to ensure that the new root system can support the new plant; it might struggle under the weight of anything larger than this.

3 Deep breath: it's time to make the magic cut. There are two different ways to do this depending on the structure of the stem. If the plant has a plain brown woody stem like a fiddle-leaf fig or rubber plant, either of the cutting techniques described below can be used, but we recommend the 'ringing' method outlined in Step 4.

If the stem has a thicker, strap-like appearance, such as *Dieffenbachia* or *Dracaena* species, or is thinner and more flexible, move on to Step 5 (on the following page).

Either way, always cut in a direction away from your hands and fingers to avoid hurting yourself if you slip.

4 This technique is called 'ringing', and involves removing the outer, more fibrous layer of bark while leaving the inner layer intact. Take your knife and make a circular cut around the entire circumference of the stem, pushing deep enough to slice only through the outer bark. Cut another identical ring around 5cm (2 inches) along the stem from the first cut.

Next, carefully make a straight, shallow cut running from one ring to the other. You can then use the tip of your knife to peel off the outer layer of bark, leaving the woody inner portion intact. You might need to go back over the cuts if they are not quite deep enough first time round. Once done, continue to Step 6 on the following page.

5 We call this cutting technique 'grooving', and it involves simply making a deep slice in the stem. It is more suitable for stems that are either too tough or too skinny to strip with the 'ringing' method.

Using your knife, carefully slice upwards into the stem from below at an angle, making the cut at least 3–5cm (1½–2 inches) in length but no deeper than halfway through the stem. This is to prevent the wounded section from snapping. Use the toothpick or match to wedge the slit open and prevent it healing.

6 Dust all of the cut area with rooting powder, making sure it reaches all the way into the slit if you have used the 'grooving' method.

7 Take a generous handful of sphagnum moss and squeeze out the excess water so that it is moist but not dripping wet. If you have used the 'grooving' method, first push some moss up into the slit section, and then encase the entire cut stem with the rest. If you have used the 'ringing' method, you will need to simply encase the stripped section of the stem with the moss, adding more until you have a good mound encircling the entire stem.

8 Keeping hold of the sphagnum moss with one hand, use the other to wrap the plastic sheet around it, securing both ends with your string or ties to keep the moisture from evaporating. The moss will trigger root growth, prevent bacteria from growing and give the roots a crucial supply of water.

9 Over the coming months, you will need to keep an eye on the moss to make sure it doesn't dry out. To check hydration and for signs of roots, loosen the tied end at the top of the bundle: if the moss is dry, pour a little water in with a pipette, jug or spoon.

10 It will likely take at least three to six months for roots to be visible, and the moss should stay damp at all times.

The roots will be delicate, so check them very carefully; do not move onto the next step until you can see a healthy mass of white roots growing – more than pictured in the photo on the bottom right (opposite).

11 Once you can see those roots, use a knife or secateurs to cut the stem off just below the sphagnum moss. If the plant you are propagating is a sappy *Ficus*, you may need a clean cloth and an elastic band to cover the cut end and prevent any mess or skin irritation. Remove the plastic wrapping and loosen the moss a little. Then, repot the plant, burying the roots and moss. Place the pot somewhere away from direct sunlight until it is properly acclimatised to its new home.

12 For the first couple of months you can water the plant gently from above or by filling its drainage tray. You want to keep the soil moist but not drenched.

Layering

Ground Layering

In the wild, ground layering can happen naturally when the shoot of a plant happens to grow down and make contact with the earth. This contact triggers the plant to try to develop a new root system in order to gather more nutrients. You often see this in nature with species of ivy, when their stems branch out and anchor into the ground, eventually sprawling around the central stem.

For the indoor gardener, this method is ideal for multiplying houseplants that have softer, more flexible stems that can be bent downwards. Some popular examples are thinner-stemmed *Ficus* species, heartleaf philodendron, *Schefflera* and *Pothos*. If the stems are thicker or more rigid, the plant may be better suited to air layering (see pages 138–143).

Pick stems that are mature enough to bend without snapping, and avoid any that are very young or showing signs of damage. Remember that not all propagation is successful, so you may want to try this method with two or three stems, in case any don't take root.

Once you have decided which stems you would like to propagate, you will need to place the mother plant in a spot that has enough space around it for the stems to be arched down and rooted within additional and peripheral pots. If you are moving the plant to a new position in order to find space for additional pots, remember to choose an area that also suits its temperature and lighting requirements.

Rooting may take up to 12 months and the pots should not be disturbed during this process, although you can inspect the stem occasionally to check root progress and that the compost hasn't dried out.

Layering

Ground Layering Method

Small pots and drainage trays
Small drainage stones
Compost (see p40)
Sharp, sterile knife or scalpel
Rooting boost, powder (see p36–39)
A few medium-sized stones

Before you begin, check that you have enough space around the parent plant for additional pots and that the surface is even – disturbing the process halfway through could damage any stems you have already cut.

Depending on the size of the additional pots, you may need to use some props such as a block of wood or stack of books to give them a little more height next to the parent plant. This is to avoid putting too much strain on the stems being propagated once they are bent downwards.

The photos on the right show heartleaf philodendron (*Philodendron scandens*), which is an ideal candidate for ground layering.

Layering

1 Fill your smaller pot or pots with a layer (a couple of cm/an inch or so will do) of small drainage stones. Top the pot up with compost, packed down gently. You may need to add a little water if it feels at all dry.

2 Select the stems you would like to propagate, choosing those that are mature enough to bend downwards and into a U-shaped curve without snapping.

3 Practise bringing each stem to its new pot and make a note of the best place to cut the stem to suit the space you have. You can also remove any leaves or side shoots along the main stem that are in the way of the curved section.

4 Taking your first stem, use your knife or scalpel to make one or two shallow notches on the underside of the curve, making sure to keep your fingers well away from the sharp edge of the blade. Don't worry if you accidentally cut too deep; as long as the stem is still partially attached, it is likely you can still produce roots.

5 Apply a dusting of rooting boost to the cuts to give them the best chance of rooting.

6 With the cut side of the stem facing downwards, bury the section of the stem under 5–7cm (2–3 inches) of compost, leaving the tip of the stem poking above. You may need to adjust the position of your pots to avoid putting strain on the stem.

Place one of your larger stones on top of the compost as a weight, to keep the stem from lifting out.

7 Check the compost every few weeks and give it a gentle water – either very carefully from above or by filling its drainage tray – to ensure that the compost stays moist but is never drenched.

8 After a couple of months, check to see if roots have formed by removing the stone and lifting the stem upwards very gently to feel for resistance. The stem will move easily if no roots have formed; cover the stem again and check in another few months or so. If you feel resistance, you know that roots have grown successfully. At this point the rooted stem is ready to live independently – simply sever the main stem from the parent plant and begin to enjoy your brand new, miniature plantlet.

Tropical Seedlings

You are my seedling
All fresh possibilities
Your roots explore the dark earth
Your head lifts to the arcing sun

Fiona Langton

Y ou can't beat the sense of wonder that comes from nurturing a
plant from seed to shoot, but many houseplants won't flower indoors,
or, if they do, are unlikely to pollinate by themselves. Cacti and other
houseplant seeds can be bought, of course, but they do tend to be a bit
tricky to cultivate without some very technical equipment.

Amazingly, though, lots of the fruit seeds we would normally throw in
the bin can easily be grown indoors, and the process is much quicker and
more satisfying, especially since you can experiment with those you happen
to gather in the kitchen. It's the perfect way to introduce kids to gardening
and, once sprouted, the tropical seedlings make really thoughtful presents.

Some of our favourite seeds that can be germinated indoors include
the avocado (look out for Hass and Holiday varieties), acorns (pick them
in autumn before they fall), lychees and coconuts, which can be planted
whole and will eventually grow into palm trees. You can even sprout sweet
potatoes by simply sitting them in a glass of water. In this chapter we have
included two favourite tropical seeds – the date and the mango – that can
be grown indoors and will mature beautifully in a pot for many years.

Before sowing any fruit seeds, make sure to wash them really carefully
to get rid of any flesh and residues. This will reduce the chance of mould
growing later down the line. Seeds from fresh fruits generally germinate
much more successfully than those that are dried or old, but all are possible
to grow from, so don't let that put you off.

If you can't sow the seeds right away, you can store them for up to three
or four days inside a grip seal plastic bag or plastic box lined with damp
kitchen towel.

Finally, a great trick to check which seeds are viable is the 'float test'.
Place the seeds in a bucket of water and leave them for a couple of hours.
The seeds that sink to the bottom are likely to germinate, but you can
discard any that float on the surface, which will not be viable.

Tropical Seedlings

Date Palms

Clean cloth
Grip seal plastic bag or plastic box
Pots with drainage trays
Small drainage stones
Compost (see introduction below)
Spray mister or watering can
Liquid organic feed (optional)

You will find that your date seeds will germinate quickly, but the seedlings will mature very slowly, meaning you can keep them potted up on display for a long time without them needing much attention. We love seeing how they change shape, at first sprouting a single blade before eventually fanning out elegantly.

Date palms like a light, well draining soil: mix two parts coir to one part horticultural sand/vermiculite or, alternatively, mix one part sand to one part tropical seedling compost.

Ideally, germinate the seeds from early spring to early summer so that they have the best possible environment to establish roots before winter. Look out for medjool and deglet noor varieties.

1 After removing the seeds from your dates, give them a rinse to remove any residues and place them in a cup of tepid water to soak for 24–48 hours. This will soften the coating around the seed.

2 Next, wet your cloth, squeeze out the excess water and fold the seeds inside so that they are all covered. Don't place the seeds too close together; they will each want their own space and water to germinate.

3 Encase the parcel within the grip seal bag or plastic box, and place it somewhere warm (a comfortable room temperature of around 21°C / 70°F is ideal) and dark. Leave the seeds undisturbed for around two to three weeks, or until you notice them sprout white roots.

4 After the seeds have germinated and the sprouts are clearly visible, it's time to plant them up. Line your drainage trays with stones and fill your pots with fresh rooting compost. Then bury the seeds on their sides, roots facing downwards, at least 3cm (1½ inches) below the surface.

Keep the pots somewhere warm, with plenty of bright light. Palms are typically native to arid parts of the world, and are very sensitive to overwatering. Aim to keep the compost just damp, but more on the dry side.

5 After about three months you should see a little sprout appear, similar to a blade of grass. From here, you can nurture your mini palm tree, repotting to a pot one size up only when the roots are pot bound. To encourage its growth, fertilise the plant with a diluted liquid organic feed (such as a seaweed-infused variety) once a month during spring and summer, but never over winter.

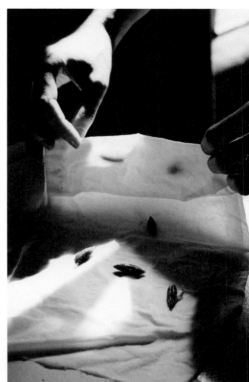

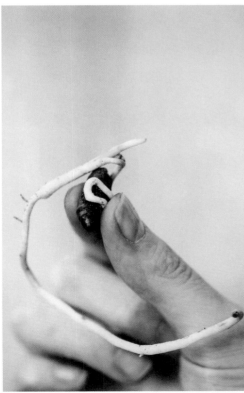

GROW POCKETS

T he designer of *Root, Nurture, Grow* – the wonderful Giulia Garbin – is a woman of many talents. During the time we spent together working on this book, we discovered her prints, including her narrative linocut illustrations.

We collaborated with her for this project to create personalised 'grow pockets' – simple pouches to gift friends with precious seeds, oxalis bulbs, succulent leaves and cactus offsets. The designs are inspired by traditional botanical etchings, which are easily found and offer endless inspiration.

Pencil and paper
Tracing paper
Sellotape
Piece of lino
Lino cutting tool
Sheet of acetate
Printing roller and relief ink
Newspaper
String washer envelopes
Cleaner and rag to clean your tools

1 Start by drawing your design on to paper as you would like it to appear on the envelope. Keep in mind that you will be tracing over the sketch for the next step, so strong outlines and graphic shading work well.

2 Next, secure the tracing paper over your drawing with some small squares of sellotape to keep them from shifting. Trace over the design with your pencil; at this stage you can make any changes to the design if you like.

3 Place the lino right side up on a hard surface, and flip the traced drawing face down on top, so that the pencil markings are touching the lino.

4 To transfer the pencil drawing, simply shade over the back of the tracing paper. Apply enough pressure for the pencil markings to rub off onto the lino. The design will now be a mirror image of your drawing, but remember that it will be reversed again when printed.

5 Use your cutting tool to carefully carve the lino around your drawing away, leaving the drawn lines intact. A good tip is to carve around the edges of the outlines first so that you can see them clearly. Carving in outward strokes from the drawn lines can also be really effective. Don't worry if you make mistakes at first – sometimes the most successful designs are those you think have gone horribly wrong!
   If it is too big, trim your lino to roughly the same dimensions as your envelope, leaving a little excess. Clean the lino of any shavings and set it aside.

6 Lay the acetate sheet down on a layer of newspaper. Squeeze a little of your ink on to the acetate, and use your roller to spread the ink out until the roller is evenly coated. Roll in vertical and horizontal strokes to blend away any lines; you will hear a tacky sound once the ink is thinly spread.

7 With your lino laid on a separate, clean piece of newspaper, roll on the ink with quite a bit of pressure, up and down the cut surface to coat the outlines of your design to apply the ink steadily. Repeat the rolling in different directions, going back to the acetate for more ink if needed.

8 To print your illustration, first place an envelope face up on a clean piece of paper. Carefully lay the lino on top, ink-side down. Then press down firmly with your hands. You can use a clean roller for this is you have one. Finally, peel off the lino and leave the envelopes somewhere to dry until you are ready to use them. You can add to the final print by repeating this process with more cut lino designs and colours if you like.
   For a little extra embellishment (and padding), try folding your seeds and bulbs inside some delicate tissue paper before sealing them inside the envelope for their new owner.

Tropical Seedlings

Mini Mango Trees

Growing a mango plant from seed is a joy in so many ways: first, you get to eat the juicy mango flesh, then you expose the seed (which is enormous and often brightly coloured), and then, after germination, you simply watch as a beautiful, pinky copper-coloured shoot emerges.

Keep in mind that, being a tropical fruit, the mango tree needs a high level of sunlight and humidity, and although it will sprout quickly you may find it tricky to grow indoors past a certain height. Aim to give it the warmest, brightest spot of your home (a south-facing windowsill is ideal) and, if possible, move it to a greenhouse once it has matured so that it has the best chance of fruiting.

You may be fine without one, but if your indoor conditions are on the cool side, a heat mat to provide bottom warmth during germination will increase your success rate significantly. As with most seeds, it's best to sow them in early spring.

Mini Mango Trees Method

Scouring brush
Secateurs
Small glass
Seedling compost
Pot and drainage tray
Small drainage stones
Cloche or clear plastic bag and string/bin bag tie

1 Each mango seed is protected inside a rough husky outer shell, which is what you normally see after eating a mango. After cutting open the mango and removing the ripe flesh, give the shell a thorough scour and clean under running water, removing as much of the remaining fruit flesh as possible.

2 Next, very carefully trim along the edge of the husk with your secateurs, taking care not to catch the seed hidden inside. Once exposed and removed, give the seed a gentle rinse to remove any sticky residues. Sometimes the seed will have germinated while inside the husk, and you will see the root already growing. The narrower end of the seed is where the root and shoot will grow.

3 Fill your glass about half full with room temperature water and sit the seed upright inside the glass, making sure that only the narrow, rooting end is submerged. Sit the glass anywhere shady and warm (a room temperature of around 21°C / 70°F is ideal).

Keep an eye on the water level over the next two or three weeks, keeping it topped up. Refresh it regularly to prevent any bacteria forming.

4 After time, you will see a root appear from the bottom, and then a little later a shoot will emerge, curl and begin to grow upwards. We normally keep the seed in its glass of water throughout this process, although you might need to move it to a bigger glass as the roots develop.

5 Once the root and shoot are established, it's time to move the seed to its new home. Fill your pot with compost and add stones to your drainage tray. Sow the seed by submerging both the seed and root in compost. If your home is cool or very dry, you can boost temperature and humidity for the first couple of months by using a glass cloche, or by encasing the entire plant within a clear plastic bag. Make sure to cut in some air holes, and fully ventilate the plant every couple of days to prevent mould growth.

6 Keep the mango's compost warm and damp, but never wet – good drainage is essential. It is best to use room temperature water when giving it a drink, to prevent chilling the plant and harming its roots. Repot annually. If pruning, avoid contact with the sap inside its stems as it can irritate the skin.

Tropical Seedlings

Cultivating

Grow old along with me
The best is yet to be

Robert Browning

Pruning

With such a wide variety of indoor plant species available to bring home, knowing how and when to prune each individual can sometimes be bewildering; the last thing you want is to cause more harm than good, or permanently disfigure a plant.

It might be reassuring to know that pruning is quite simple; except for a few types listed below, most houseplants will react brilliantly to an occasional trim. By cutting back straggly or overzealous sections, you can encourage new growth elsewhere and keep fuller areas as healthy as possible.

The best spot to cut is just above a new leaf or leaf node. Ideally, cut at a 45-degree angle, using very clean and sharp scissors, secateurs, a knife or scalpel. You may need some shears or a saw for large, woody-stemmed plants. This process will encourage bushiness by forcing the stem to produce two new shoots from either side of the cut.

If you want to plant the cutting, make sure to trim again just below a node higher up its stem. You can root this cutting in a new pot, or stick it back in the original pot to increase the bushiness of the plant it came from.

Before reaching for your knife, though, take a step back to observe the plant carefully in its position, keeping in mind the eventual shape you are hoping to create. You can then begin pruning little by little, continuing until you are happy with the overall appearance (rather than making a cut you might regret).

When it comes to timing, it is best to carry out any major pruning when the plant is in its active growth period, and therefore more resilient. You can tell a plant is active when it begins to grow new shoots, leaves and flowers, typically during spring and summer. The only exception is if you use grow lights and regulate the plant's optimum temperature, in which case it will stay active all year round.

Aim to carry out any drastic surgery as early in spring as possible, and avoid pruning at the end of summer, when the plant may not have time to restore itself before it enters its dormant phase. Dead leaves, flowers and stems can be removed any time of year to prevent mould forming.

There are certain houseplants that cannot revive cut stems, and – except for dead flowers or individual leaves – should only have their stems pruned with caution, ensuring enough healthy stems are left to sustain the plant. These include palms, ferns, snake plant, *Calathea*, *Oxalis*, *Agave*, *Aspidistra* and bromeliads.

If any of these types develop brown or damaged stems or leaves, they can be trimmed off to improve their overall look, but prune carefully; cut the stems at their base to avoid leaving parts which will eventually dry up and wither, and bear in mind that the cut stems will never regrow.

Don't forget you can recycle many cut stems and leaves to grow entirely new plants, making the most of any leftovers.

Cultivating

Pinching &
Root Pruning

Both pinching and root pruning will prevent the need
for major attention or repotting later down the line,
enabling the plant to remain at optimum health in your
chosen pot.

'Pinching' is a more delicate form of pruning that
involves removing the tips of stems to encourage
fullness and healthy growth lower down the plant.
It is particularly beneficial for begonias and ivy,
Pothos, *Philodendron* and other vine species, which
often become leggy indoors.

The key is to remove newer, softer stem growth
by pinching the tips of main and side stems between
your thumb and index finger. Like pruning, always pinch
above a node or new leaf. If done during the plant's
active growth period, this process will encourage side
buds to grow, giving the plant a boost of energy and a
better shape.

It is also good practice to look at the surface of the
compost, where many houseplants produce suckers
(see pages 128–133) and, less commonly, aerial tubers.
Although they won't harm the parent plant, these
plantlets can divert growth, sometimes causing the
parent plant's stems to grow leggy. Once they are clearly
visible, we advise gently removing these suckers and
aerial tubers and replanting them in a new pot to protect
the vibrancy of the parent plant.

Cultivating

Below the compost, root pruning is a brilliant way to keep potted plants looking their best and prevent them from outgrowing their surroundings or becoming pot-bound. The technique is useful where living space is limited, when you may want to prevent plants from expanding too enthusiastically.

It is best to combine the method with some stem pruning to make sure that the newly reduced root system can support the plant above it. Alternatively, it is a great way to maintain plants that don't respond well to stem pruning – you will find a list on page 173.

You can check a plant's roots by carefully removing it from its pot when the soil is fairly dry. If you see roots circling, clustering or forming a mass around the outside of the soil, you know it is a good time to either repot or prune them. Other signs of a pot-bound plant include roots growing through drainage holes or above soil level, a bulging pot, and reduced plant growth and vibrancy generally.

If possible, loosen the roots with your fingers to remove as much of the old compost as possible. Then, using a sharp knife, scissors or secateurs, cut away some of the outer roots. You can cut back about a third of the roots if necessary without causing long-term harm to the plant. Afterwards, replant with fresh compost, making sure to tap the base of the pot and pat the soil down as you go, so that any large air pockets are filled in. Then water the plant well, giving the soil a good soak.

If you notice the plant looking frail afterwards, use a bamboo pole and twine for extra support. And keep the plant away from harsh sunlight until it has resettled. See page 188 for more help with sudden plant collapse.

Aftercare

One minute you have a blooming, thriving plant that doesn't seem to have a worry in the world, the next, you find its leaves have browned and dropped, and it's stopped growing. All is not lost. There could be many ways to revive an ailing plant, but first you need to understand its symptoms.

To help you figure out why your plant is showing signs of sickliness, we've created a list problems you can visually identify in the plant, together with a list of causes we have found to be most likely, from classic overwatering to too much heat or fertiliser.

The the best solutions to these symptoms and causes is listed on the following pages. And on page 188, you'll find advice in the case of sudden plant collapse. The saddest case of all!

Remember that there are often various causes for the symptoms displayed by an ailing houseplant, so we recommend reading and considering each of the possible causes, as well as carefully considering the environment surrounding your plant, before dramatically changing your care routine.

Common Problems

Brown, Dropping Leaves
Too much heat · Too cold
· Too little natural light ·
Natural growth cycle

Sudden Shedding Leaves
Underwatering · Pest
damage · Sudden change in
temperature · Sudden change
in light levels

Curled Leaves
Under watering · Too
much heat

Brown, Patchy Leaves
Too much heat · Overhandling
· If patches are papery,
underwatering · If patches are
soft and dark, overwatering

Yellowing Leaves
Underwatering ·
Overwatering · Too little
natural light · Calcium
damage (from tap water)

Wilted Leaves and Stems
Under watering · Poor
drainage · Pot bound ·
Too much heat

**Pale Leaves and
Spindly Stems**
Too little natural light ·
Too cold · Underwatering
· Overwatering · Under-
fertilising

Brown Leaf Tips
Underwatering ·
Overwatering · Not enough
humidity · Over-fertilising

**White, Cotton-Wool-Like
Growths**
The dreaded mealy bugs!

**Soft, Brown or Black
Stems or Roots**
Overwatering · Too cold

No Growth
Pot bound · Underwatering
· Overwatering · Under-
fertilising · Too little
natural light

Causes & Solutions

Underwatering or Overwatering

Overwatering is the most common cause of bad houseplant health, especially for those that don't have pots with drainage holes. Check the compost by sticking a finger in to around 5cm (2 inches) deep.

If the compost is soggy, or the plant is sitting in water, pour away any excess and stop watering until the compost is dry again. Do some research to check how much water the plant actually needs and rethink your watering habits. You may need to remove any rotten stems and roots, which will be soft and brown in colour.

If the compost feels bone dry, and you think you may have neglected it for a while, give it a large cup of room temperature water to begin with, and more after a few hours if needed.

See pages 18–21 for more advice on the best methods of watering. And use a bamboo pole and some twine to support the plant while it is in recovery.

Too Much Heat

If your home is bathed in lots of natural light, then we envy you. But more delicate, tropical species will prefer a shady corner to a sunny windowsill, so check your plant isn't getting more light or heat than it needs. Try moving the plant to a shadier spot, and make sure the plant is getting enough water.

Look out for radiators and central heating units, which can cause harmful fluctuations of hot, dry air. Except for cacti and other succulents, which like as much sun as possible, most tropical houseplants will thrive with plenty of bright, indirect light, and daytime temperatures of around 21°C / 70°F.

Cultivating

Too Cold

Especially in colder months, when temperatures can fall well below the optimum temperature, many species start showing signs of deterioration. If your home gets chilly during the winter, we recommend significantly reducing how much water you give your houseplants, encouraging them into a state of dormancy. Allow compost to dry out completely before watering, and if the plant starts to wilt, increase humidity by encasing it in a clear plastic bag with holes for circulation. Alternatively, move the plant to a warmer spot, and cluster any delicate species together to increase warmth and humidity.

Not Enough Humidity

For plants that like lots of humidity (often thinner-leaved species which are native to the rainforest), try increasing humidity by filling drainage trays with a layer of gravel or small stones. Excess water can collect below the plant without directly touching the roots, and this acts as a reservoir in drier months.

You can also mist these plants' leaves regularly with room temperature water to keep them hydrated. Though to be honest, this will only make a significant difference if you have the time to do so at least once a day.

Too Little Fertiliser

Most shop-bought indoor plants come with enough fertiliser in their compost to nourish them for a few months. Once this supply runs out, your plants will benefit from an occasional feed during spring and summer months. There are plenty of organic houseplant feeds to choose from, which can be diluted by adding a little to your watering can; make sure to find out how much each plant needs first.

Too Much Fertiliser

Too much fertiliser can cause more damage than good, particularly with air plants and delicate tropical species. Check you are diluting your plant food correctly. Fertilise only during the active growth period, and always dilute it with water rather than pouring it directly into the compost.

Too Little Natural Light

Particularly in the case of cacti and other succulents, sun-loving plants will suffer over time if they are kept in a shady spot. A lack of chlorophyll can stunt growth, and you may notice plants becoming leggy and spindly in their search for more light.

Try moving plants into brighter spots of your home, observing how the light moves around each room. If your home is shady, you can invest in some grow lights to give plants a boost of brightness; the lights aren't hugely expensive and we find they help to lift the mood of people as well as plants.

Pest Damage

Luckily, most pests found indoors are easy to spot and can be carefully dealt with by using a solution of soapy water. A spray solution of equal parts water and alcohol can also be effective. Adding a layer of topdressing stones can help to prevent bugs or flies from laying their eggs in the compost. If the pests look like little white balls of cotton wool, continue reading, as the problem is most likely to be...

The Dreaded Mealy Bug!

These critters are tricky little devils since they are hard to treat and spread quickly, often affecting more than one plant at a time. The best solution is to manually remove as many bugs and egg sacks (which look like cotton wool balls) as possible. Make sure to check the undersides and grooves of leaves and stems, where they often hide. Then spray the affected areas with an organic pesticide or alcohol solution. If you can, take the plant outside and give it a thorough rinse to wash off any you may have missed. Keep checking the plant regularly and re-treat as needed.

Check the roots of the plant too, as mealy bugs can lay their eggs deep within the compost; the problem won't be solved unless you get rid of these too. Isolate the affected plant during treatment, and if you think the plant is sadly beyond saving, make sure to dispose of it quickly before it spreads to any other plants, which should be checked carefully too.

Cultivating

Pot Bound

Every couple of years, the roots of an actively growing plant will outgrow its pot, diminishing the nutrients in the compost and stunting growth. To check whether your plant needs to be repotted, wait until the compost is fairly dry and carefully remove it from its pot. If you can see the roots circling around the outside of the compost, you know it is time to repot. You may also notice roots escaping from the pot's drainage holes.

Unless the roots are extremely dense, pick a new pot that is only a little wider than the original. This is to prevent the plant from going into shock in its newly spacious surroundings.

Over Handling

If a plant is touched a lot (we don't blame you), or is in a position when it regularly gets brushed against, you might find more delicate leaves showing signs of damage. Try to resist the temptation to handle the leaves too much, and consider moving it to a more protected space.

Natural Growth Cycle

Just like any living organism, your plants will replenish themselves as they develop, growing new leaves and eventually shedding older ones to conserve energy. If you think your plant is getting the right level of water and warmth, then simply prune brown, shrivelled leaves by gently pinching them off. Dead leaves should come away easily, so if the leaf shows resistance it might be best to stop and reconsider the cause of the problem.

Calcium Damage

If you live in an area where the tap water is hard, limescale can eventually build up and cause plant damage. A simple solution is to replace tap water with rain water: place a bucket outside your home and decant rainwater into your watering can. Your plants and plantlets will be so much healthier for it.

Reviving a Plant

We've all experienced the shame: suddenly, a once-poised plant will flop, drop its leaves dramatically and give you a look of despair.

Rather than an enigmatic pest or disease, the most likely cause of sudden plant collapse is an extreme of one of its fundamental needs: temperature, water and light. You may be too late to rescue it, but it has the best chance of survival if you can identify the cause and make changes, pronto.

Before you take drastic action, cut off a piece of stem to check for signs of life; if the stem is very crisp and dry throughout, then your plant is most likely a goner. However, if the stem is remotely moist or green inside, there's hope yet...

First things first: check the room temperature. A particularly cold winter's night or sudden heat from a vent will damage your plant very quickly, especially delicate, tropical species. If you think this is the cause, move the plant to a more suitable spot.

Another likely cause is drowning or drought, both of which will eventually damage a plant's roots beyond repair. Check the soil to see if it feels either very dry or very wet. See pages 18–21 for more advice.

Finally, check if the plant is receiving an extreme level of natural light, either not enough or too much. Some plants will collapse when newly exposed to direct sunlight, and others will eventually succumb to limited natural light even if they have seemingly coped for many months beforehand.

Our final tip to save a collapsed tropical houseplant is to use a bamboo pole and some twine to support the plant, and then encase the whole plant in a clear plastic bag, which will act to increase temperature and humidity while it restores itself. Make sure to give it some ventilation, and, once it has perked up, slowly acclimatise it back into your home.

FLOATING JUNGLES

O nce you've filled every possible uninhabited surface in your home with greenery, we recommend embellishing the ceilings with leaves, too.

Inspired by Matisse's leafy silhouettes and the sculptures of Alexander Calder, these hovering copper mobiles are delicate and simple to compose. They look most elegant suspended from a ceiling hook where they can waltz in the air.

This project requires a few purchases, but chances are you'll find many of the basic materials in your home. We have included two options for materials to choose from: finer sheets of copper can be cut with scissors are much easier to assemble, but the thicker copper gives a more impressive finish. You'll need a pair of tin snips or metal cutting scissors for the thicker copper.

As copper can react directly with plants, you should use non-reactive string or invisible fishing wire to hang your mobile from a sturdy plant stem. Alternatively, you can simply hang it delicately on a ceiling hook.

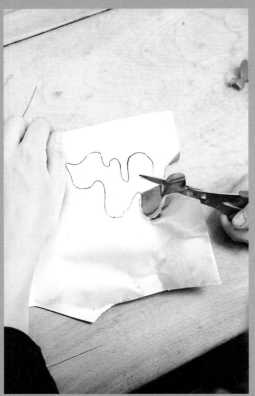

Pencil and paper
Hanging thread or fishing wire
Soft cloth
0.1–0.3mm (0.04–0.1 inch) craft copper sheets
1.4mm (0.55 inch) copper wire
Scalpel and cutting board, scissors or tin snips
Long-nose pliers
Thick needle and thumb pad

1 Start by looking at the plants you have in your home and pick some with bold, interesting leaf shapes. We have chosen our favourite wiggly fishbone cactus for this design.

2 To make templates of your leaf shapes, start on paper, either drawing by eye or by taking cuttings and drawing around their silhouettes. If a plant's stem is long and flexible, you may be able to draw around the leaf without cutting it from the plant; if not, remember you can always plant the cutting up once you have finished the project.

3 Cut out as many paper templates as you would like. Then lay the shapes out to experiment with scale and arrangement. To transfer the designs to copper, simply trace around the templates with a sharp pencil and then cut them out with scissors (or a scalpel and knife, if you are using the thicker copper sheets). Use long, smooth strokes to create clean lines. Take care handling the cut copper, which can be sharp at the edges.

4 Once all your copper shapes are cut out and you have an idea of how you want to arrange them, use your needle to pierce a hole at the top of each shape.

5 To start assembling your mobile, cut a length of wire and use your pliers to make small u-bends at the ends; leave them slightly open at this point so that you can attach and switch the copper shapes later, if needed.

To make the first, lowest tier of your mobile, begin with two of your copper shapes, attaching them to either end of the wire where the u-bends should keep them in place. Then, shape the main length of wire into an arched curve by running it between your fingers.

6 Balance the curved wire on your finger to find a sweet spot where it naturally hangs; this is the point to attach the next section of the mobile. Use your pliers to carefully shape a loop in the wire at this balancing spot (we recommend practising looping first on some spare wire). Don't worry if the sweet spot is not at the centre of the wire; this is because the copper shapes are different sizes and weights, and as you continue you will find everything evens out once the mobile is hung.

Cultivating

7 For the next tier of the mobile, replicate Step 5, this time attaching just one copper shape on one side, and leaving the other u-bend free to connect to the balancing spot of the first tier. You can rub the copper shapes on a surface with a soft cloth to smooth out any dents or bumps as you go.

8 Make a new, small coil of wire by looping a 5–10cm (2–4 inch) length around your pliers. Leave it quite loosely coiled. Feed this coiled wire through the balancing spot loop of your first tier, and then tighten the new loop of wire to secure it. Hook this new loop onto the u-bend of the second tier, which will create the next tier of the mobile.

9 Continue in this way, finding the balancing spot of each new tier as you go, and making new, separate loops of wire to connect them. You can keep extending your mobile or keep it quite small and simple. On the final tier, repeat the step of finding the balancing point and creating a loop in the wire, and use this as the point from which to hang your mobile.

While You're Away

As fulfilling as relaxing at home with your houseplant family can be, there will inevitably come a period of holiday when they must be left behind unattended. If you don't have anyone to help you while you're away, the uncertainties of how they will cope in your absence can be worrying. Luckily there are some simple ways you can prepare them before you leave, minimising changes to their environment and putting your mind at ease.

Summer Holiday Care

During warmer months, indoor plants are much more active in their root and stem growth, and therefore require significantly more water to survive. Leaving them unattended for a prolonged period over spring or summer months can become problematic, especially for tropical species of plants that are not used to sudden periods of drought.

If you are lucky enough to have a friend who will pay a visit, make sure they are aware of the biggest houseplant killer, which tends to be overzealous watering.

If not, before you leave, shift the plants away from any direct sources of light or heat, such as south-facing windows or radiators. Add a layer of small drainage stones to each plant's drainage tray, which will increase humidity below the pot and reduce the chance of dehydration. Then give them a generous watering; any excess water will simply sit in the reservoir created by the drainage stones.

Alternatively, use a capillary mat to line a large drainage tray; this absorbent material can be saturated with water before you leave, and will allow a steady supply of water to your plants. Sitting your plants on a bed of thick, soaked towels in a bath will work in a similar way.

If you are going away for longer than a couple of weeks, we recommend removing any new buds or flowers, which can require a lot of energy.

Our self-watering pot project on pages 114–119 is another option; the plant will simply take up as much moisture as it needs from the pot's inbuilt reservoir while you are away.

Cuttings & Propagated Plant Babies

During the early stages of propagation, when delicate root systems are beginning to develop, young cuttings are particularly vulnerable. Too much or too little light, water or heat can damage them beyond repair.

Aside from the suggestions above, investing in a capillary mat can provide a brilliant solution. Otherwise, we recommend placing the plantlets within a plastic bag tied at the top to reduce water loss.

Winter Holidays

During the winter, most houseplants will enter a dormant state and require little or no water. As long as you can keep your home from falling below the minimum temperature they require, and you leave the plants with moist (but not drenched) compost, you should have no problem.

Never leave plants on cold windowsills over winter, and never repot or fertilise them either.

You can give your plants some extra care by grouping them together in the warmest and brightest spot of your house, away from draughty doors or windows.

Index

Index

Index

Acknowledgements

To our brilliant team: photographer Erika Raxworthy, commissioning editor Zena Alkayat, designer Giulia Garbin, copy editor Laura Nicolson and illustrator Karl-Joel Larsson; working with you all has been a pleasure. A special thank you to Erika for her styling skills and for helping us shape the look of Ro Co over the past three years; Erika, your ability to find hidden beauty is exceptional and we will miss you greatly. But what a great excuse for a research trip to California!

To Heather Holden-Brown, Charlotte Bufton and Matt Doyle for their guidance, and to Samuel Keyte and Petor Georgallou for continuing to be happy(ish) to help.

We reached out to some talented designers who generously donated and lent us their creations to play with. Thanks to Niwaki, Okatsune, Serax, Ikea, and Iris Hantverk for donating us beautiful tools, to Andrea Roman, Emma McDowall, Libby Ballard, Louise Madzia and Matthias Kaiser for their awesome ceramics and pots, and to Rebecca Gladstone and Fran Regan for jazzing up our weathered hands with their bespoke jewellery.

We also discovered many wonderful locations: thanks to Chelsea Physic Garden and Rye Studio in London, and Curve Roasters in Margate. We're especially grateful to Vanessa da Silva from House of Two Door, photographer Steph Wilson, interior stylist Laura Fulmine and Liam and Louise from The Reading Rooms in Margate for welcoming us into their studios and homes.

Special thanks to David, Carly and Ayshea from The National Botanic Garden of Wales for their generosity and for the magical backstage tour. Also to hydroponics expert Gareth Hopcroft for continuing to share his specialist knowledge with us.

Finally, thank you for buying this book. You can follow our video tutorials, propagating experiments and styling inspiration through our website and Instagram. Please visit www.ro-co.uk.

Caro & Rose
Ro Co

Useful links

www.botanicgarden.wales
www.chelseaphysicgarden.co.uk
www.house-of-two-door.com

www.ryelondon.com
www.thereadingroomsmargate.co.uk
www.ecothrive.co.uk